"An enlightened analysis of ~~examining the seven types of negotiation tensions. A~~ ful dive into being a successful negotiator."

Arnold Donald,
(former) CEO of Carnival Corporation and PLC

"As a professional poker player who negotiates high-stakes deals at the turn of a card, Cash's work has given me a new command over my game."

Kenna James,
20x Las Vegas Poker Champion

"Negotiation is ultimately a human enterprise, and this book has keen insights into how to use the seven tensions to achieve better outcomes."

Andrew D. Martin,
Chancellor, Washington University in St. Louis

"One of the best guides to successful negotiations in the past decade. A must-read for practitioners and academics alike."

Tom Meredith,
Partner, Brightstar Capital Partners

THE SEVEN TENSIONS
OF NEGOTIATION
AND HOW TO
Master Them

CASH NICKERSON

MADE FOR SUCCESS

Made for Success Publishing
P.O. Box 1775 Issaquah, WA 98027
www.MadeForSuccess.com

Distributed by Made for Success Publishing

First Printing

Library of Congress Cataloging-in-Publication data
Nickerson, Cash
   The Seven Tensions of Negotiation and How to Master Them
   p. cm.

   LCCN: 2024944403
   ISBN: 978-1-64146-894-7 (*Paperback*)
   ISBN: 978-1-64146-851-0 (*eBook*)
   ISBN: 978-1-64146-852-7 (*Audiobook*)

Printed in the United States of America

For further information, contact Made for Success Publishing
+14255266480 or email service@madeforsuccess.net

Table of Contents

ACKNOWLEDGMENTS

SUCCESS AND FAILURE share one thing in common. They are both team efforts. It is an unfortunate human tendency to add others to our failure team and take a solo bow at success. This book has been a successful project, with its progress spanning over three and a half years. It has simultaneously been a thesis, although the book has a modest bibliography and the thesis has over one hundred footnotes. I particularly want to thank my thesis advisor and academic coach, Professor Karen Tokarz. Besides being the Charles Nagel Professor of Public Interest Law and Public Service, Professor Tokarz is an international legend in the negotiation and dispute resolution field. She personally has mediated over 1,000 disputes and founded and supported numerous public interest groups to benefit the underprivileged. Professor Tokarz has supported my teaching efforts at WashULaw since 2018 and was an early reader who helped provide input to my previous negotiation book, *Negotiation as a Martial Art*.

For this book, she arranged academic opportunities for me to present material and take on rigorous questions. When I needed encouragement to improve my work, she did so in a kind yet candid way. So, thank you, Professor.

Secondly, I want to thank the students I have had in the classes I have taught at WashULaw. I have taught Business Lawyering since 2018, and the Introduction to Negotiation class for 1L's since 2021. Whoever said you don't know a topic until you teach it couldn't be more right, in my opinion. These WashULaw students are among the top law students in the country, easily ranking in the top five schools for entering LSATs and GPAs. They push and test everything put forward and have made me a better teacher, a better listener, and a better negotiator. Between those two teaching experiences, I have had over four hundred students. Thanks to each of you for your attentiveness, engagement, and commitment to negotiation and dispute resolution.

Cash Nickerson

INTRODUCTION

Why Focus on Tension?

I HAVE BEEN fascinated by martial arts for virtually my entire life. I love internal martial arts the most, but I also love to attend boxing matches and UFC fights. The internal martial arts focus on internal energy and the power from breathing, mindfulness, meditation, relaxation, and flow. In contrast, the external martial arts are what you see when you watch a UFC (Ultimate Fighting Championship) or martial arts contest. The highest-level martial artists use their internal training to perform at extraordinary levels externally. I recall flying back from Manchester, England, in 2016, where I had attended the UFC 204 mixed martial arts event. Seated next to me was a coach of many of the US fighters. He muttered to himself for a chunk of the flight. Intrigued, I asked, "What happened?"

He replied, "Good question. What happened? Not one of my fighters won. I trained them over and over and over.

And yet, as soon as they get in the ring, they just do what they want."

I had to say, I recognized the issue.

At that time, I was teaching and training several martial arts. I reflected on the difference in training between three of the martial arts: American Kenpo Karate, Brazilian Jiu Jitsu (BJJ), and Systema, a Russian martial art.

Training karate involves techniques and *katas*.

With BJJ, you learn various techniques, but the art is not reduced to those techniques. In BJJ, you have to feel the other person in order to know what you might want to do next. In order to feel someone else, you have to not feel yourself, so you have to relax. If you are not relaxed, all you feel is your own tension. If you are relaxed, you can feel their potential movements before they actually move.

In Systema, there are no techniques. Systema works with your instincts. If I threw a punch at you, you would do something, even if you were untrained. For example, you would try to move out of the way, but you might hold your breath or wince. So, to train in that art, you work with a person's natural response and improve it. You train them to breathe better, move better, and feel no tension. These two teachings seem to stick much quicker and much longer than others. Remove the tension and reinforce the natural instincts.

While marital arts got me focused on tension, I very quickly applied the principles I learned in the internal martial arts to business and life in general. In my business life, I have been involved in hiring hundreds, if not thousands, of employees in a staffing company I co-owned and co-managed for many years until we successfully sold it. Different clients had different "tension" cultures. Some companies, or units of companies, were high-pressure, results-driven production environments. This was common among our defense contractor clients like Boeing and Lockheed Martin. Other company cultures emphasized creativity and sought to reduce workplace stress, encouraging naps, games, and informal engagements in collaborative spaces. This culture was more common among tech company clients like Apple. In retrospect, I don't think humans perform better under stress, and recent studies call into question the high-pressure environments and parallel my observations regarding internal martial arts. In a recent study from 2023 on the association of stress with cognitive function among older black and white US adults, researchers found that perceived stress led to cognitive impairment.

In my early career in BigLaw, a common nomenclature for large law firms, the work environment was extremely tense for young associates who were expected to work sixty to eighty hours per week and be at the office seven days a week. At the time, there was a common belief that increased pressure and stress produced better results. We now know the opposite is true. Stress and tension do not help with cognition; they hurt it.

Every time I see someone negotiate, I can see the tension. Now, my professional life is focused very narrowly on negotiating for myself and, instead, on representing others in negotiations, studying, and teaching negotiation. As a relaxed individual, I can *feel* the tension of other participants in a negotiation. As a professor, when I provide students with a simulated negotiation, I can see the tension as they work to reach a deal or resolve a dispute. This shouldn't be surprising. Sitting down to negotiate, starting a Teams or Zoom call, or entering a mediation and speaking to a mediator is like getting ready to throw or defend against a punch.

I wrote extensively about tension in my most recent book, *Negotiation as a Martial Art*. In my martial arts, I was trained to silence tension within myself so I could feel the tension of others. I was trained to feel, assess, neutralize, and respond to tension. I was not trained to avoid it.

People who avoid tension might not make the best negotiators. People who seek a "win, win" solution might not make the best negotiators, either. In this book, we will assess how conflict avoidance disrupts one's ability to effectively negotiate. Please note that, in my vocabulary, conflict is external and tension is internal, the latter the result of the former. There is such a thing as good tension. Good tension instructs us, and we are conditioned to handle it. If I sense pain, I work to avoid the condition causing it. Without training, if I am in a BJJ match and someone twists my arm, I will tense up and increase the tension, making the pain worse. If I relax in response to the tension, I can draw on my training to release the tension. But I must successfully feel the tension first in order to know I have to move myself, and I must react to it in a calm way. Maintaining our analogy, understanding the tensions of negotiation helps me adjust my behavior to successfully maneuver in any negotiation.

Good negotiation involves tension. My work over the past forty years as a negotiator, both as a principal and intermediary, and my teaching and studies over the past seven years have led me to study the tension of negotiation and break it down into seven components. Being aware of the seven tensions, knowing when to expect them, and knowing what tactics or moves are most likely to counter them will allow you to reverse the negotiation and gain an advantage. When we train this way, we are working with a trainee's natural tendencies and instincts to make them better. We can trot out and train on concepts like, "You should be a good listener," but that won't really change behavior. On the other hand, suppose I can show you relationships that tend to challenge listening skills and increase tension. With that training, you will feel the tension, recognize the causes, and pivot your behavior in a way that advances listening. Instead of ignoring the tension you feel, you get in touch with the discomfort and ask yourself why. You become curious and lean into the tension instead of shying away. Wouldn't that be interesting?

CHAPTER 1

Understanding the Importance and Role of Tension, Trust, and Collaboration in Negotiation

IMAGINE THE MOST basic of negotiations, with just you and one other person. Imagine you walk through a door into a conference room with a conference table and two chairs on either end. In the room, there is another person whom you may or may not know. They are seated at the far end of the table. In the middle of the table is a Snickers bar. Next to the Snickers bar, there is a shiny table knife on a plate. There is a note on the table in front of what is presumably your chair. You sit down in the chair and read the note. The note says, "The Snickers bar in the middle of the table is for you and the person seated across from you." After you read the note, you look up at the person across from you. What do you do? How do you feel? Teasing out your likely feelings, concerns, and anxieties, you likely have the following tensions:

1. Who is the person at the other end of the table? With whom am I negotiating? Do I know them? You will have tension about the person, and I call this **Relationship Tension**.

2. What do I want? What will I get? How much of the Snickers bar should be mine? What do I deserve? What makes me entitled to it? What is my claim? You will have tension about your rights and obligations regarding who should get what, and I call this **Outcome Tension**.

3. How are we going to decide who gets what part of the candy bar? What are the rules of engagement? Will we talk to each other? Will we take turns arguing about who should get what? What if we can't decide right away? Should we schedule a follow-up call or meeting? What should we do with the candy bar in the meantime? You will have tension about how to decide who gets what, and I call this **Process Tension**.

4. How long do we have to perform this sharing exercise? What other time commitments do I have? How about the timing of the person across the table? How long does the candy bar last? You will wonder how time is a factor, and I call this **Timing Tension**.

5. Is the person on the other side of the table stronger, smarter, or more powerful than me? What does she or he know that I don't? What if they just take it? Does either party have the ability to influence or control the other? You will worry and have tension about your relative strengths as you sit there. I call this uncertainty **Leverage or Power Tension**.

6. Is there someone who can advise me or work on my behalf? Do I need an intermediary to help me? As I sit and ponder my situation and all the other tensions, I have to wonder whether I am in over my head. Can I handle this, or do I need some help? Or am I in the room on behalf of someone else? Whether you need help or are helping someone else, you are facing what I call **Agent Tension**.

7. Who else would benefit from sharing my candy bar? Is there a family or team involved? Is it my decision to make, or do I have to get permission, approval, or consensus from others? Is there a company policy on how I should approach the negotiation? Who else am I supposed to consult? As you think thoughts like this, you are experiencing **Team Tension**.

What is the very next thing you do? Should you speak first? Should you just split the candy bar in half? Should you engage in chitchat before talking about the candy bar in the middle of the table? Should you brainstorm all the reasons you should get more than half of the candy bar? Maybe you didn't have breakfast. Maybe you can convince the other person that the candy bar is unhealthy and that you are doing them a favor by eating it all yourself.

Your mind will race to think of the possibilities, probably before you have even asked yourself whether you like Snickers bars. If you have taken a course in negotiation, you may begin to think about "win-win" scenarios. Maybe there will be other candy bars, and they can have this one, and you will get the next one. Maybe you read *Never Split the Difference* and start looking for potential tactical empathy opportunities, like a common enemy. Who are these people who put us in this room to deal with this issue? How dare they?

Suppose, instead of wading through the swirling tensions, you could master them. Suppose by sorting the tensions and learning how to master them, you could quickly and efficiently resolve the candy bar problem. Suppose while the person on the other end of the table was feeling everything described above—with their palms sweating, heart beating quicker, and brain under stress—you calmly analyzed and applied techniques to resolve the tensions fearlessly and without regret.

The thesis of my book is that all negotiations involve tension, specifically, the seven tensions I described at the beginning of this chapter. Learning to segment, understand, and manage tensions rather than avoid them is critical to our ability to negotiate successfully with each other. I believe that even when we teach negotiation, we too often teach tension avoidance techniques to gain a "win-win" scenario rather than teach how to manage tensions in a head-on and transparent way. With the ability to identify and segment the seven tensions and an understanding of the tools to ease those tensions, you will master every negotiation you encounter.

Tension, Trust, and Collaboration

Imagine a relationship you have with someone very important to you. This could be a husband, wife, child, partner, business associate, close relative, or even a pet. Reflect and be honest with yourself about the variety of interactions you have with this person. Sometimes, the interactions are frustratingly tense. Sometimes, they are a beautiful collaboration. Sometimes, great collaborations follow tension. Sometimes, tension becomes a permanent impediment to interaction. But in your best relationships, don't you find a way to move from tension to collaboration, sometimes even leveraging the tension? It is fair to ask why some interactions successfully move away from tension while others do not. Additionally, can we learn how to move from tension to collaboration and back again when appropriate? Can we manage the pendulum, or does it just swing randomly?

If it is a long-term and successful relationship, it likely involves a high level of trust. Trust is the lubricant that allows parties to move easily from tension to collaboration. With trust, the time between tension and collaboration may be remarkably short. If it is a new and developing relationship in which there is very little trust, the time between the highs and lows may be longer. How can we build trust? Can we use science and the arts to help us improve the dynamism of this dialectic, this back-and-forth between tension and collaboration? If we can do that, we can improve how we negotiate with each other. If we can improve how well we negotiate, we can change the world.

The Cost of Negotiation Incompetence

Negotiation is a basic human activity that arises out of wants, needs, and disputes. I want something you have. You want something I have. We want the same thing. I want to trade you this for that. I think you owe me something. You think I wronged you, and now you want me to pay you damages.

We join in interpersonal unions and relationships based on how well we negotiate with each other. As organized collections of people, we negotiate terms of exchange, terms of labor, and conditions of interaction. We do this commercially through companies and collectively as nations. When we can't sort matters commercially, we litigate. When nations can't resolve differences through negotiation, wars erupt. In the US alone, large companies in 2021 spent $23.71 billion on litigation. How do we measure the human cost of war? In the one hundred years of the twentieth century, 231 million people died as a result of wars. What are we doing to reduce the corporate waste from litigation expenses and the loss of life from conflicts?

At the end of 2023, we witnessed the consequences of a failure to negotiate a solution to the Israeli/Palestinian conflict. To be sure, progress toward a two-state solution was happening, which, according to some, led to the brutal October 7, 2023 attack. Clearly, we took too long.

In another instance, Putin amassed one hundred thousand troops on the Ukrainian border and created tension around the world. What did we do? We did nothing. Were we paralyzed by the tension? Suppose we broke down that feeling of tension into its seven components. What would that look like? We had relationship tension: Vladimir Putin, a dictator, showed in Crimea that he had the will to follow through on his threats. Putin bargained through leverage, which is another of our seven tensions. Was I the only one who saw his amassing of force as a request to negotiate? I once heard retired Three Star General McMaster speak, and someone asked him what he would have done. He said he would have amassed tanks along the Ukrainian border in response. That makes sense. As a tank commander who understood Putin's style, he would have responded in kind: leverage against leverage. He would have used what he knew from the relationship tension to respond in a way his counterparty would have understood—by applying leverage tension.

At a minimum, you would think we would have engaged in a negotiation. Watching with tension was not a deterrent. There was evidence in the early peace talks that if Ukraine had not agreed to join NATO, then Russia would have stopped fighting, and peace would have ensued. Had we broken down the overall tension into the seven tensions, we would have realized that Putin was asking for a response, determined an acceptable outcome for us and the world, and reacted according to the leverage tension presented.

And instead of negotiating, we watched. Tensely.

The Benevolent Negotiator – *Getting to Yes*

One of the most prominent repositories for the study of negotiation is the Harvard Negotiation Project (1979) at the Harvard Law School, which shares its roots with the fundamental book on negotiation, *Getting to Yes*. This book, first published in 1981, introduced the concept of principled negotiation. The authors of the book, Ury and Fisher, were the original co-chairs of the Harvard Negotiation Project. Their book provided an alternative framework to positional negotiation. Positional negotiation, it posited, was about fighting. Positional negotiation was a battle of tensions. You got what you wanted by pushing harder, using power, wearing people down, and advocating more effectively. Their book sought to provide an alternative to pushing and shoving.

Getting to Yes built principled negotiation on four major pillars. Principled negotiation was about 1) separating the people from the problem, 2) getting underneath positions to discover underlying interests, 3) inventing options for mutual gain, and 4) using objective criteria. It wasn't as though no one was doing these things in their actual practices, but this was the first and most notable attempt by academics at a university to put them together in a detached way. It was an intellectual and structured framework that could be used by practitioners to support their practices, training, and negotiation culture. It became *the* framework. Virtually all books since have felt compelled to pivot off of it because it was the first fundamental attempt at intellectual structure to the negotiation topic. The Program on Negotiation (PON) has proliferated, and every year, it offers thousands of people certificates upon completion of training in the way of *Getting to Yes*. It's a big deal. The authors are treated like the founders of a religion.

As satisfying as the principled negotiation framework is, it is more appropriate to canned simulations than real-life negotiations. I worked to overlay the bifurcation of the perceived

"Neanderthal method" of positional negotiation over the beautiful and idealistic world of principled negotiation with my own forty years of professional and personal experience and couldn't get the pieces to fit.

I am a rare person who has straddled academia and practice. To be sure, I have had more time in practice. In my forty years, I have been a corporate lawyer in the law department of a multi-billion-dollar company, an associate, and then a partner at a large law firm based in Chicago, a business executive, an entrepreneur, a CFO, and a CEO. I have seen negotiations from every facet you can imagine. On the academic side, I have taught a class on negotiation to law students at Washington University School of Law (WashULaw) since the Spring of 2018, and I am a JSD student at the school. I have written several books on the topic, including, most recently, *Negotiation as a Martial Art: Techniques to Master the Art of Human Exchange* (Made for Success, 2021). As you can see, I have a multifaceted perspective.

My experience, perspective, and research have shown that successful negotiation is not so simply principled, and not all positional negotiation is bad. Instead, negotiation is a dialectic, of sorts, with a swinging pendulum moving from tension to collaboration back to tension. The academic work on *Getting to Yes* and its progeny has been helpful but oversold. Getting stuck on something creates tension. Until you resolve that issue by working through the tension, you won't have progress. Progress and tension often go hand in hand, and you can't have one unless you can work through the other. The notion of a collaborative utopia being the be-all, end-all would be nice, but it doesn't comport with reality or science. As I was recently describing my Snickers bar scenario to a law professor and explaining the problem with collaboration being the end-all, she said, "I get it. We teach negotiation as if someone might say, 'You take the wrapper, and I will take the candy bar,' and the other person would say, 'Great, I need a wrapper.' "

As extreme and silly as this sounds, in fact, in *GTY* itself, they offer a similar example by decrying the splitting of an orange between two children, when in fact, one wanted the orange and one wanted the peel. Do you know any children who really want the peel to make a pie? I have coined the phrase "Jack Sprat Fallacy" to reflect the mistaken belief that your counterparty will really want the lesser of the split. Do you really believe that Jack Sprat's wife only liked to eat fat? Don't underestimate your counterparty's desire for precisely what you want.

Tension Avoidance as a Negotiation Culture

This has profound implications for how we teach negotiation to students, employees, and other constituents and how we approach negotiation as a culture. To further complicate matters, telling students to collaborate has its own challenges. What does "collaborate" really mean? When was the last time we taught collaboration? Moreover, most negotiation work is done by teams. How much time do we spend teaching internal and external collaboration? We teach students negotiation principles to avoid tension and to collaborate, but we know this isn't the path to successful negotiation in our own lives. We know we will have to deal with tension.

Let's return to your close relationship where we began, and consider the important role of tension. Once people experience tension, then temperatures and blood pressures rise. Tempers might flare in high-tension areas. Adrenaline kicks in, and stress elevates. In healthy relationships, there is a resolution, or there is a deferral until there can be a resolution. Without that tension, arguably, nothing would happen. The question, then, is not about how to avoid tension but how to understand it and its relationship to collaboration. How can we learn and teach the smooth movement of the pendulum between the two? How can we actively manage the dialectic? As you add parties or participants to the dialectic, matters like trust and influence play a strong role in managing the tension.

If we are going to address tension rather than avoid it, we need to understand it. As with understanding many concepts, the key is teasing it into its various components, which I have spent years doing as I've studied and taught. Separating tension into its constituent seven components—relationship tension, process tension, leverage/power tension, timing tension, outcome tension, team tension, and agent tension—and learning and acquiring tools to address and manage those tensions is the key to negotiation success.

Drawing on negotiations, transcripts of negotiations, social psychology, linguistics analysis, applied math, and systems theory, I will show the importance of positional bargaining and the role of the seven tensions in the progress and resolution of disputes, mostly in commercial negotiations. The academic notion that one should pursue principled negotiation, not positional negotiation, is just that, academic. The under-standing of and the ability to manage the relationship between tension and collaboration is critical to negotiation success, and we need to retool our education to train students on how and when to move from one to the other. When should they bring the Yin, and when should they bring the Yang? If we can do that, we can reduce the negative and costly social consequences that stem from our failure to seek, find, and resolve tension by mastering the dialectic it has with collaboration.

CHAPTER 2

The Seven Tensions

THROUGHOUT MY EXPERIENCE, I have identified the seven tensions that appear in most negotiations.

The first involves the relationship between the negotiating parties. Are you strangers, fiduciaries, or long-term partners? Different relationships lead to different tensions, but regardless, the tension is real.

The second tension is the outcome of the negotiation. What will you get, and what do you want? What will they get, and what do they want?

The third tension is the process of the negotiation. How will you get from here to the outcome? Will you have one session or several? Will you deal with all the topics at each session or just some? Will you exchange emails, meet face to face, use Teams or Zoom, or call on the phone?

The fourth tension is timing tension. Great dealmakers say, "Timing is everything." What does that mean?

The fifth tension is leverage or power tension. Who has the power in the situation? Who has the greater Best Alternative to a Negotiated Agreement (BATNA)?

Do you have an intermediary? Are you the agent of another? If so, there is agent tension, our sixth tension of negotiation.

Finally, are you on your own or part of a team? How coherent is that team? If it is just you, how coherent is your mind? How is your internal team? This tension, team tension, is the seventh tension. Learning these tensions so you can recognize them is the key to becoming a great, fearless, regretless negotiator.

Relationship Tension

Imagine how different the Snickers bar negotiation would be depending on the identity of the person at the other end of the table. Let's consider a few different scenarios. First, suppose it is your worst enemy. Second, suppose it is your best friend. Third, suppose it is your spouse, significant other, or your child. What if it is someone who is starving? What if it is your boss or someone else who controls your happiness, pay, or benefits? Relationship tension will affect your outcome and process desires. It will probably affect your desire or willingness to use leverage. Will there be an ongoing relationship with this person, or is it a one-time transaction? Not all of us will adapt in the same way to these relationship variances. You might split the Snickers bar in half with the enemy and give the entire candy bar to a child or someone who is starving. No matter how you would react, it's important to explore this tension to get to a result that you won't regret.

Process Tension

How will you determine what to do with the candy bar? What is the first thing you will say when you sit down? Will you wait for them to say something? Should you engage in some chit-chat first to get to know the other party? If it is your enemy, how will you protect your interest? What will you do if the other party picks up the candy bar and the knife and says, "Come and get it"? How you approach the process of deciding who gets what will likely determine the outcome. Exploring the process is critical for reaching a satisfactory agreement.

Leverage/Power Tension

Suppose the other party has the knife and the candy bar when you walk into the room. Suppose, instead, you walk up to the candy bar and take it and the knife. Suppose the person on the other side is your parent or boss, and they say, "You aren't getting any of this candy bar; you didn't earn it." Much of negotiation has to do with leverage and force, but you won't find that in books that teach "win-win" negotiation.

Putin amasses his forces on the Ukrainian border. Do you separate the people from the problem as suggested by *Getting to Yes*? Or do you use the seven-tension relationship analysis to determine that the person *is* the problem?

Timing Tension

Ask a good-deal lawyer or business-deal maker about negotiation tactics, and they are likely going to say, "Timing is everything." Where can we find that in modern negotiation instruction? If timing is everything, why can't we find it in *Getting to Yes*?

In January 2021, Zelensky tried to join NATO and froze the assets of the Kremlin's most powerful and prominent ally in Ukraine. In the Spring of 2021, Russia started to mass troops on the border. By November 2021, satellite photos showed that the mass of troops likely exceeded one hundred thousand. In February 2022, Russia invaded Ukraine. What did the US and NATO do between January 2021 and February 2022?

Leaving the political realm, let's consider commercial transactions. Suppose you want to buy a new car. Your time frame is important. Do you need one today or sometime in the next six months? How about the dealer or salesperson? What is their timing need? Are they short on sales for the month and need to move another car today to make a quota? Is there a sales contest, and can the salesperson win if they sell a car in the next three days? Your timing and their timing matter to the negotiation.

Outcome Tension

The outcome tension is the primary tension that parties address. Do you want the whole Snickers bar? What do they want? *Getting to Yes*, for example, is founded on this basic tension. Let's revisit the four pillars of the book.

Separate the people from the problem. In other words, focus on what outcome you want and not on the people in the room.

Focus on interests, not positions. Get behind the position so you can understand and work with the underlying interest. If someone says they want something, try to understand their motivation or the "why" behind it. What outcome do they really want?

Invent Options for Mutual Gain. Find some outcomes that are win/win. What is your best alternative to a negotiated agreement?

Finally, *use objective criteria.* In other words, you need to know what other people generally get and have a standard defensible basis for the outcome you want.

All of these only focus on one of the seven tensions—outcome tension. This is the primary shortcoming of *Getting to Yes.* In its attempt to avoid positional bargaining and promote collaboration, it misses six of the seven tensions.

Team Tension

Any substantial commercial negotiation will involve a team. Teams make you question how to best divide duties, responsibilities, and accountabilities. Additionally, you have to consider how well everyone gets along and who is ideally on your team. We usually think of people with charisma, good personalities, and high EQs as better negotiators. But studies don't necessarily show that. In fact, some studies show they get worse results than tough negotiators. But who does the best? A sequential team of a competitive negotiator followed by a cooperative negotiator leads to the best results. What a surprise: bad cop followed by good cop works. So, how you pick your team matters, as does when and how they play. There will be team tension between the good cops and the bad cops, even if that is the best combination.

Agent Tension

Many transactions involve intermediaries. When working with an agent, there are a few important things to consider. What is the impact of an intermediary? What good do they do? What harm can they do? How can you tell whether they are truly working for you? Are they a partner, an advocate, or a team member?

Suppose I enter the room and see an enemy or someone I don't like on the other side of the table. Then, I leave the room and send in a representative. I have resolved my relationship tension but introduced intermediary tension. Now, the representative returns an hour later with part of the candy bar, except I notice it is in two pieces, one larger than the other. He gives me the larger piece and says, "Hey, look what I got you." It appears to be about a third of the original bar. He says, "Well, when the other party saw you got an intermediary, she decided to get one. We worked and worked, and eventually, we split the bar in half. The other representative and I have a fee of one-third, so I am taking fifteen percent of the bar, which leaves you with thirty-five percent.

Congratulations, you probably could have done a fifty-fifty deal with your enemy.

CHAPTER 3

Relationship Tension

RELATIONSHIP TENSION IS at the heart of many negotiations. The nature of the relationship between the negotiating parties affects how one should approach virtually all other tensions. It affects the outcome, leverage, and how one might use that leverage. It affects process tension.

Let's return to the Snickers bar example. Look at the impact of two different types of relationships on this situation. With your worst enemy, you may quickly split the difference so you can get out of the room as quickly as possible. Your feelings toward the enemy party affect your process tension ("Get me out of here!"), your timing tension (how long you want to spend on this), and your outcome tension (whatever will be the quickest solution that leads to the least interaction). The tension with your enemy might also affect your agent tensions ("Let me give it to someone else") and cause team stress. The hostile counterparty lights up all of the other tensions, doesn't it?

Let's contrast that relationship with a warm, close personal tie. What if you are negotiating with your child? Instead of lighting up all of your tensions, they may make them disappear. Now, you want to make sure your child has everything they need. You don't want an agent, and you will be dismissive of any interference from your team. Your outcome tension will be driven by sacrifices.

Once you understand the extremes, you should be able to recognize that the relationship really matters. Any notion of separating the people from the problem or even disentangling the two does not align with how we live our lives.

On the first day of class, I ask my students to write about a negotiation experience they have had. I specify that I want a real negotiation, not just how they would handle an imaginary simulation. I don't care if it was as small as buying a used book or as large as buying a used car. I employ this assignment to start getting them into the habit of reflecting on negotiations for purposes of improvement and corrective action (outlined in Appendix C). I also use it to help them practice the art of listening because I pair them up during class and each student has to listen to the other very carefully. I don't allow them to take notes, and they have to recount the story just from memory.

One time, a student recounted selling a piece of furniture to another student. While it wasn't feasible for the selling student to deliver the furniture herself, she agreed to do so because she knew she would see the buying student in the hallways and didn't want her to be upset in any way with the transaction.

In commercial relationships, you see this often in merger and acquisition environments. If you are buying a company and you need the current owners to be involved, you will want to form a good relationship with them. This will likely affect the other tensions. The process will be "softer" to preserve the relationship. There may be fewer timing pressures. The outcome may be more favorable, although it will likely be tied to performance in the post-deal relationship.

If the relationship doesn't affect the buyer or seller in a transaction where there will be an ongoing relationship, that should be a red flag to the seller. The buyer might be giving you a snapshot of their culture and seeking to acclimate you to it as part of the transaction. If it feels cold, you might be getting insight into what is to come. The message also might be that the acquirer doesn't plan for you to be a part of the company for very long.

If you already know the other party, you can start asking yourself a few helpful questions: What is your experience with them? What behavior do you expect based on your past experience? Do you hold any biases based on previous encounters? Part of the power of a post-negotiation review is that you can record your interactions with counterparties and use them to prepare for your next encounter. However, you must carefully toe the line between reasonably prepared and biased. Bias based on past experience can be given too much credibility. According to Thin Slice Theory, our impression of someone is often based on a very quick reaction. So, take a beat. You must consciously fight your powerful, immediate impression or, at least, be skeptical of it.

Existing relationships may be the most fitting situation in which to apply the *Getting to Yes* mandate of disentangling people from the problem. I agree that we should at least disentangle biases we hold based on previous behavior. That doesn't mean we ignore everything we observe; we just need to be careful not to reinforce biases that were not carefully constructed. This is perhaps where human behavior in relationships is at its weakest.

Suppose your significant other has made it clear that they think you carelessly spend too much money. You, on the other hand, harbor a belief that your significant other misses out on some experiences and has less fun due to their frugality. Suppose that, one day, you are discussing where to go to dinner, debating between a steak house or a pizza place. You are, of course, negotiating. You suggest the steak house, which is more expensive and much further away. Your spouse says he is fine with pizza. Then, you immediately launch into a tirade about your partner being cheap. Yet, your partner wasn't thinking about money; he was just hungry and wanted to eat sooner. In this case, you have effectively "pre-crimed" your partner based on beliefs you have discussed before. (The term "pre-crime" came from the 1956 book by Phillip K. Dick called *Minority Report,* first published in Fantastic Universe and later made into a successful movie with Tom Cruise.)

To avoid pre-criming and excessive bias when negotiating with a counterparty(ies) you know, ask questions and employ active listening. A simple question such as, "Why do you want pizza?" may have drawn out the actual reason without resorting to unnecessary criticism.

But what if you don't know the counterparty(ies)? If I don't know my counterparty, my very first, very important task is to find out everything I can about them. Why? I can't use the Seven Tensions of Negotiation as well if I don't know the counterparty(ies). I need to know their underlying motivations and true interests to find alternatives. I need to know how they operate to steer the process of resolving our differences to get our deal done. I need to know how they will respond to timing tension. I need to know their team and community. I need to understand their leverage. Knowing who they are and forming a relationship with them is critical to every other tension.

Your first goal has to be to find out what you can about the counterparty(ies). There are so many tools for this. If you are negotiating with a company, you can search for their website, their competitors' websites, their LinkedIn, and who you may be dealing with from the company. Who do they know that you know? Who are the common friends or followers you have with them? This research is critical to your investigation. Finding a common friend or "link" can lead to a treasure trove of information that can help you more successfully negotiate with your counterparty(ies).

Once you find a common link, you need to be prepared to ask them structured questions. Appendix D provides you with some suggested questions about your counterparty and your common link. You need to know that there is a risk that the common link will tell your counterparty(ies) about any and all conversations you've had. You can try to manage that by asking for confidentiality, but depending on your common link, that may not be realistic. As a result, you should tailor your investigation around the reality that your inquiry and its scope may reach your counterparty(ies).

You can conduct some of your investigations secretly. LinkedIn has settings that allow you to be anonymous when searching for someone. I personally don't mind that someone knows I looked at their LinkedIn profile, so I am visible. If anyone mentions it to me, I simply comment that I consider it part of my homework for doing a good, thorough job for my client. I also will compliment them about something I learned from their profile, like an award, honor, or other achievement.

Once you refresh your recollection of the parties you know or do your research on parties you don't know, you can and should use this information to reduce relationship tension. This can be especially helpful in the early stages of the negotiation process. Thin Slice Theory shows that we make snap judgments about others, meaning the first few minutes of a negotiation are critical to its success. At the Advanced Master Class at the Harvard Law School, we spent lots of time practicing the first one hundred eighty seconds of a negotiation under the tutelage of Professor Brian Mandell.

I also noticed this same behavior over six thousand miles away in Istanbul. Great negotiators work to establish rapport and know it is critical to do so in the very first moments of the negotiation. How long the rapport-seeking phase lasts may vary from culture to culture. In some cultures, it may take several rapport meetings before anything approaching trust is established.

The information you have on your counterparty(ies) can be used to establish common bonds. Based on your research or knowledge, find common interests with your counterparty(ies). These can be the foundation of early discussions. In business circles, you will likely be able to find some connections.

The information you obtain or already have on your counterparty(ies) can help you manage the seven tensions. Knowing how aggressive a counterparty or their agent is can help you prepare your negotiation plan. Knowing how they approach the negotiation process can be helpful as well. Do they operate remotely, or do they prefer face-to-face? The preparation planning in Appendix A will help you take the information you have and turn it into a solid negotiation plan.

Lastly, there are many other parties in and around a negotiation worth considering. These can be allies, adversaries, influencers, commentators, reporters, and observers. Allies are groups or people who support you and your objectives. For obvious reasons, it's important to identify your allies. You can potentially draw on them for support in your negotiation. Adversaries are obviously important because they can be brought in as allies of your counterparty(ies). Influencers may just be folks on the sideline, but they are in a position to sway the parties, their allies, or adversaries. Commentators are people or groups who are likely to share opinions on the topic of the negotiation with observers and reporters, perhaps commenting in a newspaper or other media source. Reporters are similar to commentators, but I use the term "reporter" to mean someone of more neutrality. Finally, there may be observers who express interest in the negotiation, and these people could move into one of the other categories. You even need to be aware of them if you can be.

Let's consider an example that includes all of these parties. Suppose an employee in their sixties is laid off by a company, and the employee files an EEOC complaint against the company for age discrimination. The parties are the company and the employee. Allies of the employee may be other older workers in the company and the EEOC itself. Allies of the company (adversaries of the employee) may be other companies in their industry, the law firm representing the company, and younger employees in the company who are hoping positions open up for them. Commentators could include law firms looking for older clients to represent in similar cases. Reporters might be legal blogs and periodicals. Observers could include other lawyers sitting on the sidelines to see what happens, as it might generate work for them. All these parties are keenly interested in what is going on with the negotiation and could play a role. Observers, allies, and adversaries might become active. Once a single employee files a complaint, others may follow, for example. You might decide to resolve the complaint quickly to avoid others becoming involved. Paying attention to the relationship environment and the risks and opportunities it presents is critical to determining how to handle the negotiation.

Assessing and understanding the relationship you have with your counterparty or parties is critical to every other element of a negotiation. Building rapport is a recognized step in all negotiations, even positional negotiations with perceived enemies. If you know the person or company, then make sure you consider it in your approach. If your counterparty is new to you, then conduct thorough research. Finally, allies and adversaries can play a role in helping or inhibiting your negotiation. As with all tensions, you must be aware that they can change and, therefore, must be approached with the dynamic awareness of an organic development.

CHAPTER 4

Process Tension

PROCESS TENSION IS the tension at the beginning of a negotiation journey that comes from all the strategy, planning, logistics, agent, and team decisions. In some ways, it is reliant on all the other tensions because when you plan, you have to think about the who (relationship tension/agent tension/team tension), the what (outcome tension), the when (timing tension), and the differences in power (leverage tension).

In my experience, process tension does not have a lot of coverage because negotiators do not spend adequate time preparing for a negotiation. If you don't prepare, your process will be to arrive at a meeting with some notes about what you or your client wants. However, the best negotiators I know are obsessed with process tension and preparation.

Designing the Journey

Designing the process means documenting your plan. Using a template (or predetermined set of questions) will ensure you don't have gaps in your plan and that you cover issues that may arise due to the seven tensions. It's imperative to consider the relationship, leverage, and timing issues, as well as understand the potential changes in tension that can happen over time. Moreover, by using the same preparation template each time, you can check yourself midstream and reflect on the negotiation afterward. The template can become your work papers to help assess if you are on track or not. I don't prepare for a negotiation of any kind without using a template. A template will remind you of each move you made in a negotiation and help determine what is working with this counterparty and what is not. It can help you improve your skills, predictions, and outcomes. I have created a template of questions based on the Seven Tensions of Negotiation to assist you in preparing for any negotiation. You can find it in Appendix A.

Selecting the Lead/Leaders/Roles

One of the most important aspects of process tension relies on relationship tension and considers who should be in the negotiation. Who should be on the team? Who should lead the team? What roles should you include in the room?

This doesn't just apply to the beginning of the negotiation; it is also applicable as the negotiation unfolds. Changing who is in the room or changing out negotiators can be a very strategic move. This aspect of a process plan can be changed very quickly. You may change the relationship aspect of the process by bringing someone with a more agreeable style into the negotiation to break a deadlock, or you may just want to clear the room to avoid "performances," as I had to do in one condo HOA negotiation.

Like most real estate, condo buildings are built by real estate developers. The Uniform Condominium Act, which has been adopted by fourteen states, allows developers to file a declaration to create a condo building, and under that same law, it is stated that after three to five years, the condo building will revert to the owners of the units. During that transition, often called developer turnover, the common elements cease to be the responsibility of the developer and turn over to the owners, who also take over the board of directors of the corporation that owns the building.

Unfortunately for owners, there is no provision in the law for an inspection at that point. This leaves the owners vulnerable to problems with the commonly owned elements. These elements include not only gyms, conference rooms, libraries, movie rooms, and ballrooms but also the mechanical and structural components of the building, including the roof, the water systems, the electrical and gas systems, and sewer and refuse systems. As anyone who owns a home knows, there is always something going wrong when it comes to mechanical or structural home components, and that is exacerbated when all of the systems are in one place. Therefore, at turnover, the resident owners will typically request an inspection for the components and hold the developer accountable for any items of concern.

At one building where I was an officer on the board, our inspections uncovered some issues that needed to be addressed. We told the developer what we needed based on our experts' opinions and then worked to negotiate a financial resolution.

In this type of negotiation, you always want to make sure you get enough money to handle the issues. We had a board of four members, and each of us had a very different style. We had a very practical gentleman who was a DIY type and, therefore, seemed to have "hands-on" experience with virtually every type of home-related system. We had a very savvy female entrepreneur who was a very careful, spend-conscious, but value-driven contributor. Lastly, we had a very tough former investigative journalist who, after reflection, made up her mind and then found a way to get there. Additionally, our lawyer was a highly competent construction lawyer. Not much in the way of compromise.

The developer's team was full of lawyers. There was a lawyer for the developer, another lawyer represented the builder, and yet another represented the systems engineers. Some of the lawyers had younger associates with them. It was a very full room. A lot of our negotiations took place with sixteen people in the room. I led our team as VP, CFO, and Treasurer (and unofficial legal counsel). The other side was led by the developer's representative, but negotiations were really led by the builder's lawyer.

We were pretty much at an impasse when I got a call from the other side's lead, suggesting a meeting as soon as possible. When you are at an impasse, you should always take the meeting. We met, and the lead lawyer for their side said, "We have finally gotten our insurer to step up, and they have an offer for you. It is $XXX." Finally, the number was much higher than previous numbers and in a range that we could settle, pay for our issues, and potentially have money left over. I immediately called for a break as soon as we heard the offer. We hadn't met for five minutes when I asked for a break. Never be afraid to take a time-out to meet with your team. Doing so allows you to make process-related adjustments, like changing who is in the room or changing the topic of discussion. You can use these breaks to assert control over the process either with the counterparty or with your own team.

My team met separately in another room. Everyone was pretty happy except for our tough negotiator. She wanted more, and I didn't disagree with her or dismiss it. After all, it would be unusual for the insurer not to have some additional dollars above their initial offer. I said I was happy to pursue it but wanted to do it privately with just the lawyer for the building. I wanted to avoid performances on the other side. With large groups of lawyers, you won't be surprised to know that they sometimes like to compete for who is smarter, tougher, better looking, etc. Everyone on my side readily agreed.

We discussed the amount we wanted to aim for, and I went off to find their lead lawyer. Their team was meeting in another area of our building. I interrupted them and asked if I could meet alone with their lead. They also agreed. Once we were alone, I told their lead lawyer that we were indeed close. I asked him if he had a little more so we could reach our goal. He said he wasn't sure. At this point, I had gotten to know him a little bit, and I believed him. He thought it would take him an hour or so to contact the insurer and find out. About twenty minutes later, he found me and countered our counteroffer with exactly what we wanted. We shook on the deal.

Then, we all met again so we could share the good news and thank everyone for their support in getting the matter settled. My strategy of negotiating the final offer with their lead alone was successful, and I knew we had done the right process as a couple of the other lawyers started criticizing the deal. But it was too late. The insurer was coming up with the funds, and we had settled. Had we not left the big room for the final negotiation, we would not have settled.

Never underestimate the power of controlling who is in the room. This should be thought through carefully. It is especially critical in multi-party negotiations.

For example, I was admitted to The Harvard Program on Negotiation Advanced Master Class in the early summer of 2022. For one assignment, we completed a multi-party negotiation simulation. This assignment had one critical difference from all of the other negotiations we practiced. In each group, the instructors picked one of us to be a spoiler. I was selected, along with five others from the group of sixty participants. The spoilers were some of the best negotiators in the room, and we were tasked with trying to prevent a deal from happening within our respective negotiations.

What I learned from that exercise was as long as I could keep them in one room, I could use their interests against them. The parties were aligned on some issues, but there were direct conflicts with others. If Party A wanted the very same thing that Party B wanted, I would emphasize this problem while they were all in the same room. This would exacerbate tension and cause them not to see their common interests. It was fun to create and exploit this tension. But if they found a way to get in a breakout room, they could focus on both their differences and areas where they were aligned. They could build coalitions and make compromises. As a result, when I was left behind, as I was when they could get in a breakout room, I lost power as a spoiler. They didn't know I was a spoiler, and it wasn't obvious, but they would naturally try to seek time with various parties to compromise on this or that. If I wasn't in the room, I couldn't prevent the compromises.

The Physical

Your physical location during negotiations affects your ability to control the process tension. Studies show a benefit in face-to-face meetings when it comes to interactions, especially where creativity is involved. In negotiations, the ability to generate creative solutions is a critical component. While the pandemic gave us a chance to experience almost exclusively virtual communication, a study by Jonathan Levav, a professor at the Stanford Graduate School of Business, showed a side-by-side comparison of those who worked face-to-face and those collaborating over Zoom. Those who worked face-to-face generated fifteen to twenty percent more ideas than those operating over Zoom. Further, the quality of the ideas was better face-to-face.

If it were true that virtual communications are an equivalent method of communication for business, business travel would not have returned to the same level as pre-pandemic business travel. While business magazines predicted that business travel would be forever changed, in fact, it has returned and is projected to exceed pre-pandemic levels in 2024.

Whether a negotiation should be face-to-face or not depends on several other tensions. What is the relationship? How important is the outcome? How much confidence do you have in your agent? What does your team want? Is time a factor? What is the leverage situation? Non-verbal communication is very powerful, especially when breaking down someone's tone from their words. Three-dimensional body language is used to convey and exchange lots of data. (The literature on this is driven by the original study by Albert Mehrabian with Wiener (1967) and Mehrabian & Ferris (1967), which claimed that 55% of communication is body language, 38% is the tone of voice, and 7% is the actual words. But Mehrabian emphasized this was only in the context where nonverbal and verbal communication cues were not aligned.) Being in a room also allows you to observe how others react to someone. We tend to teach people to focus on the speaker and pay close attention to them. Of course, I do that, but I spend a substantial amount of time in a meeting or negotiation observing the reactions of the others in the room to the speaker. It is like counter-surveillance. To take it one step further, you can then observe the speaker's reaction to the reactions of others in the room.

Note that this affects your seating choice. For a negotiation, you should always sit so you can maximize your observational capabilities—not just of the speaker but of the other participants as they react to the main speaker. If you sit in the corner in a front row seat where the chairs are forward facing, you have both a good look at the speaker as well as the reactions of almost everyone else as you look back at those seated behind you.

Look at the various other tensions and how they might impact your desire to be face-to-face or not. If you have the power, you may want to flex it by requiring or suggesting a face-to-face at your office. If you don't have the power, you may want a face-to-face to gain empathy or further develop the relationship.

For example, my partner and I were in play to sell a business to a company headquartered in Europe. They asked us to come to a meeting in Paris. The meeting was held in a private room in the George V, the famous Four Seasons in the heart of Paris just off the Champs-Élysée. We shared fine wine and some of the most incredible food you can imagine while we talked about possibilities. There were multiple courses of food, along with a perfect French wine (or two) paired with each course. As we walked back to our hotel, we were hooked. It was a powerful move by a powerful prospective purchaser. We had other options to sell to companies in the US, but after that meeting, why would we do that?

I have plenty of examples where I suggested a meeting when I was perceived to be in a weaker position. For example, I was once negotiating an employment dispute with a plaintiff's lawyer. In my first response, I suggested a meeting in their town. They were shocked and said, "Are you suggesting we meet in person?" That is how unusual meeting face-to-face is for this type of dispute. It was a discombobulating suggestion that actually seemed to shake them up a bit. And while it never happened, when I would mention being in Chicago, their "fear" or tension from a face-to-face tended to lead to progress on the phone. It was clear they had a method of proceeding, and a face-to-face meeting was inconsistent with the process they used in their legal "factory."

Information Flow and Controls

Negotiation parties often don't spend enough time thinking about their information-sharing strategy. Will you flood them with data (overfill), drip it out (Wikileaks), or strategically engineer data and information sharing to assist you with negotiating? The release of information is a vital part of your process tension strategy.

Overfill

I use an overfill strategy when I know the information is overwhelmingly in my favor and I think I can change their position by getting them information. I was faced with an employment dispute with a long-term employee. The employee had some good years but had fallen in love with one of his direct reports and failed to inform us. Once that happened, it led to a breakdown in trust, and further, due to the distraction and their attempts to hide their tracks, their performance suffered dramatically. Because this employee had at one time been so valued, we overlooked incident after incident and problem after problem. Of course, other employees were aware of the relationship and felt the favoritism that the "dating" employee was getting. It was our fault, in part, because we let it go on too long. It was a mess. When we finally did address the issue through a termination with proposed severance, the employee hired a lawyer who promptly threatened to sue us.

While we had not acted swiftly enough, we had kept impeccable records and write-ups on the employee. The employee had a thick file. When the lawyer sent a letter about suing us and began to request information, I decided to help him with his discovery. I called him and said, "Let's save some time. Why don't you come to our offices, and I will give you every relevant part of his file."

He said, "Really?"

I replied, "Of course! If this goes forward, you will be able to get it through subpoenas anyway."

He arrived, and I literally gave him everything we had. I had reviewed the material, and it laid out a story that was pretty damaging to the complaining employee. I put his lawyer in a conference room. After two hours, he called me and wanted to chat.

He said, "I can't believe you waited so long to fire him."

We sat down and worked out a deal that was less favorable to the employee than what we had first offered by way of severance because now he had to share it with his attorney. When I have overwhelming evidence, I don't hesitate to "share" the volume to my advantage.

I have also seen negotiators overload information as an impediment. I remember my first case when I joined the Union Pacific Railroad as a corporate lawyer right out of law school. We were in a high-stakes dispute with a pipeline company. The pipeline company needed to cross the major railroads to lay its pipeline across the United States and had essentially called meetings with the railroads to ask for permission. Each of the railroads had a unilateral right to refuse to deal with the plaintiff pipeline company, but they could not "conspire" together, or it was a conspiracy in restraint of trade, a federal antitrust violation. The pipeline had cleverly put the railroads in one room, and during breaks, the railroads, of course, spoke with each other. It was a clever setup. We were sued along with other railroads for alleged monopolistic activities for over a billion dollars. After trebling damages under antitrust law, the survival of the railroad was threatened. However, we believed that, through discovery, we would find evidence that they had intentionally entrapped the railroads.

I remember showing up for discovery on one of my earliest business trips. The pipeline company was headquartered in San Francisco. Four of us made the trip to go through their documents (back then, they were all physical documents). We entered a warehouse they had filled with their boxes of documents, and we had to go page by page through each box. I would guess there were over one thousand boxes. I remember thinking, *What a great strategy to smother us with information.* The case settled not long afterward as, among other realities, discovery in the face of overwhelming documents proved challenging, expensive, and unsustainable.

Wikileaks

The opposite strategy is to starve your counterparty of information. Let them "curse the darkness," as they say. This is a common strategy in litigation and many deal negotiations. In litigation, generally no information is exchanged except through legal process (i.e., depositions, subpoenas for documents, and requests for admissions). Even in the context of these requests, parties will try to provide as little information as possible in response to these legal methods of compulsory process. And it starts much earlier. Corporations lawfully adopt document retention policies that allow them to destroy business records over set time periods as a normal course of business. For example, you may have a policy that all emails are automatically deleted after six months or a year. Having a document retention policy makes it less likely that a business will have documents for discovery requests.

In the transaction world, these exchanges occur through the due diligence process. On the acquisition side, for example, deals follow a generally accepted path of identifying, sourcing, filtering, initiation, due diligence, letter of intent, more due diligence, definitive agreement, more due diligence, closing, and execution. Negotiations are strongly correlated with due diligence. But what is due diligence?

Due diligence is a term that came out of the Securities Act of 1933, which held firms who promoted investments liable for their activities but exempted them from liability if they conducted due diligence. In other words, as long as they had done adequate research on the company they were buying or buying the stock of (commonly called "the target") and disclosed that research, they were exonerated from liability if there was a later issue with the company or investment. The theory is they shouldn't be responsible for something they didn't or, more importantly, couldn't know about.

In a merger and acquisition context, due diligence is the exchange of information between a buyer and seller of a company or other assets. Sellers are required to disclose material matters affecting the company through the purchase agreement itself. The purchase agreement will contain lots of representations about the company. Many of these representations will be made orally early in the purchase process. When someone buys a company or assets, they will want to know that it exists, that it is owned by the people selling it, that it doesn't have any claims they don't know about, and that the financials on the company are accurate, to name a few. The representations will stipulate that, for example, "There is no litigation affecting the company or its assets other than as set forth on Schedule A." If there is any litigation, it must be listed on Schedule A; otherwise, the seller will be in breach of the agreement when it is discovered.

Engineered Flow Control

Unlike during my youth, nowadays, in any deal of significance, there will be a virtual data room where all material information that may be requested of a company or may be in the representations will be posted. The buyer will have a due diligence checklist that states what documents or information it requires. The data posted in the data room will generally be organized around the checklist. This process is very engineered. What is disclosed, how it is disclosed, and when it is disclosed are all negotiated as part of the due diligence process.

As you consider this aspect of the process, you should have an engineered approach to information exchanged in connection with the negotiation. Most parties do not have a plan for this as part of their negotiation; they just think about it as it arises. You can have a real edge if you have thought through this in advance.

One factor you must take into account when it comes to information exchanges is that a principal is subject to legal restrictions regarding torts like fraud and misrepresentation. A lawyer is subject to the Model Rules of Professional Conduct, which governs their behavior regarding disclosing and failing to disclose information in connection with negotiations.

Timing Tension and Process Tension

Part of planning your process depends on the negotiation's timing. In a public market scenario, timing will be driven by stock prices, regulatory agencies, and internal compliance requirements. Year-end, tax-motivated transactions can cause a deal's process to be accelerated. In a non-commercial context, like a criminal trial, prosecutors often want the negotiation to move quickly before their case becomes stale as witnesses lose interest and evidence fades. The correct process from a timing perspective also includes how many and how long your sessions should last. As you can see, there are many ways in which timing becomes a pivotal factor when planning your negotiation process.

While there is no right answer for how to time a negotiation, it is important to think through various scenarios and the consequences of following different potential strategies and tactics. I recall a transaction from my younger days as a lawyer. Our client was purchasing major assets in the Midwest from a foreign firm. The foreign firm was losing money in the US operation at a harmful pace. Once we learned this, we decided to "slow roll" the negotiation. This worked very well for us because, as time moved on, they lost money by the day and, therefore, began to concede faster.

Do your best to learn about your counterparty's timing needs. They will often disclose this early on in the deal. If they don't, you should ask. Remember, timing tension can change as circumstances change.

Power Tension and Process Tension

You can use process tension to drive or take away power, and you can use power tension to dictate the process. One of the most effective ways to neutralize power advantage is to get uniform agreement on a process. Similarly, you can use your power to dictate the process.

Suppose Elon Musk or Mark Zuckerberg want to buy a company. Who do you think dictates the timing and process of the transaction? Of course, they do. When Elon Musk was buying Twitter, he immediately dictated the process via text to the CEO and Chairman of the Board.

For a weaker party, getting sign-off on an agreed-upon process reduces the power imbalance. A strong letter of intent that dictates what will happen and when, even though it is non-binding, will have the effect of corralling the stronger partner.

I was representing a small business in a transaction with a very large business. The large business didn't care about timing or about the things the small business required. They did not care about the issues the small business might have in proceeding forward. I advised the small business to get a letter of intent in front of the large business and dictate what was needed and when. This is a great power move through process because it tends to level the playing field. People often work through the process without considering how it started. When in doubt, take control of the process. Once you do, you will have greater power than ever before.

Process Tension Conclusion

Process is a critical aspect of any negotiation. You should always make sure you have a good process planning template. Be tactical when selecting representatives who will be "in the room." Once you are "in the room," you will need to decide on so many other elements of the process, e.g., in person versus remote, your place or theirs, and how you will share information. Process planning also addresses timing tension within process planning. How many sessions will you have?

How long will they last? How soon do you want to be done? Finally, process has a strong relationship with power. You can use process to curb power, and powerful people often wield their power to dictate process.

Forgoing planning your process is like trying to cut down a tree with a dull axe. As President Lincoln once famously said, "Give me six hours to chop down a tree and I will spend the first four sharpening the axe."

CHAPTER 5

Power/Leverage Tension

WHAT IS POWER and leverage in a negotiation? Several types of power have been identified in negotiation, but most academic descriptions define power as the degree to which you have a good or better BATNA. At Harvard, the Program on Negotiation staff recently described three types of power in negotiation: lack of dependence on others (corresponds to BATNA), authority power, and psychological power. Additionally, understanding and using the seven tensions opens up a whole new understanding of power in a negotiation and exposes the dynamic nature of power. After understanding traditional thinking about power, we will explore power from the perspective of the seven tensions.

Comparative BATNA

Anyone who has had any training in negotiation is aware of the term BATNA (Best Alternative to a Negotiated

Agreement), which was coined by Fisher and Ury in their 1981 book *Getting to Yes*. Your BATNA is simply what you would do if there were no deal with your counterparty. It also provides you with a reservation point (the line you shouldn't cross) because the *GTY* theory states that if you can't exceed your BATNA, you shouldn't make a deal. Instead, you should pursue your BATNA. A simple example will help explore these concepts.

Suppose you are buying a car. You are negotiating with a salesperson to buy a new 2024 Audi Q5, and they are asking for $59,000. You have found another one online at another dealership for $54,435. This is your BATNA because it is the lowest price of the car you want with the same options. With confidence, you haggle with the salesperson, but you can't get her below $56,000. You say thank you and head to the other dealership because your reservation point and your BATNA tell you to do so mathematically. Your reservation point specifies that you should not exceed $54,435 because you can simply go to the other dealership.

It is imperative that you qualify your alternatives because you run some risk in exercising your BATNA if you haven't. Suppose you head over to the other dealership and the salesperson there says, "Yes, we have that car, but it won't be here for another two months." Or the salesperson says, "We sold that car yesterday, and we are updating our systems today." Alternatively, it could be that the price was a bait price to get you into the dealership. Now you might be thinking to yourself, *Why didn't I share my BATNA with the salesperson from the first dealership and show them the ad?* They might have known what was really happening. Or maybe they would have matched the price.

Having other confirmed alternatives (BATNAs) means you are not dependent on the deal itself. In the world of mergers and acquisitions, we often say, "If you have one buyer, you have no buyer." If you are selling a company with only one buyer, negotiating concessions or getting a higher price can be hard because you lack choices. Your BATNA is to not sell the company. Ideally, several buyers will bid up the value with various alternative structures and options.

So, in our example, what is the source of the car dealer's power? They have choices. They have lots of customers who will visit the dealership that day. It is likely they have more choices than you. They also have information you don't have. They have data on what the average customer will pay for a Q5. You likely have fewer choices, and you certainly have less information. There might only be two dealers of that particular car that are available to you, and, as a result, you may only have one real BATNA. The more choices you have, the more power you have because you can simply walk away.

Authority Power

Authority power is the simplest form of power. It is the power of "because I said so, and I am the boss, commander in chief, parent, or other recognized authority figure in some recognized hierarchy."

Authority power is not a common form of power in negotiations. If you have such disproportionate authority, then is it really a negotiation? When a child asks for a car for the evening and then attempts to negotiate for the time he or she needs to be home, are they really negotiating? By my definition at the beginning of the book, they are, but since the parent has absolute authority over the car, they can just say no at any time. Therefore, in practice, authority is not power as much as a technique that can be invoked to *exercise* power. The parent parries and quibbles with the teenager and maybe has some fun and creates tension. But if the teenager crosses the line, they can simply bring the hammer down.

Likewise, in a workplace, there are degrees of authority. The CEO is accountable to the Board but has power over everyone else. Decision-making is delegated according to a power grid. This doesn't mean there are no daily attempts to negotiate a different outcome, but it is more like lobbying than negotiating. You can try to get your authority figure to do what you want, but in the end, the authority will decide what happens.

However, authority power is not always absolute. There are rebellions, mutinies, protests, and other threats to authority power. Collective bargaining is a legitimate structure that counters authority power. For example, the president of a car manufacturing company has authority over assembly line workers but is subject to the union contract. The president's authority is regulated by that contract and by governmental authority, the NLRB, and the courts.

Psychological Power

Psychological power comes from *feeling* powerful. Studies show that feeling powerful can be as effective as being powerful. You have likely seen this strategy in poker when someone plays their hand as if they are dominant and have incredible cards. Maybe they do, or maybe they don't, but they exude power and authority. Psychological power can be influenced by the full panoply of physical interactions. They might dress up or walk confidently. They might speak authoritatively. By feeling powerful and presenting themselves as powerful, they get things they otherwise might not.

The Seven Tensions and Power Tension

Now, let's consider power from the perspective of the seven tensions. Relationship tension relates to authority power. What power you have over your counterparty or what power they have over you needs to be part of your analysis of the relationship.

Outcome tension is also related to authority power. If you have power over the outcome, the question is, how much? You and your counterparty's power over the outcome should be analyzed as part of your negotiation preparation.

Timing tension has an interesting dynamic. The ability to control timing or understand the impact of timing on power does not relate to any of the traditionally recognized sources of power. However, the ability to modify timing is critical to outcomes. Imagine you are buying a house. Suppose you have ten days to do your due diligence and request changes. That is power. You can decide again in those ten days whether you want to buy the house or reprice the deal by requesting lots of repairs. Sellers want that time period to be as short as possible, and buyers want it as long as possible. This is timing power unrelated to the sources of power identified above.

Process tension is the ability to dictate what happens and how it happens. Process tension is about who is in the room and the order in which matters are addressed. I may have authority power, but, at the same time, I might be subject to process tension. I may have the power to make a decision but can't control the process it has to go through. A person may have the authority, perhaps, to home-school their children, but the state can dictate the what and how.

My team tension must be analyzed. I might have authority, but I also need to consult with others on the team.

Finally, if I have an agent or I am an agent, my power or my agent's power will be a defined term. Adding an agent to the mix could change the power dynamics.

As we will discuss in a later chapter, understanding the interplay between the power associated with each of the seven tensions is critical to flipping the script on your opponent. Likewise, understand that the power associated with each of the seven tensions is dynamic and changes over time. An understanding of the trajectory of each of the tensions, as well as the interplay is what will make you an advanced and superior negotiator.

Traditional power analysis means you have power because you have better BATNAs, authority, or psychological power. However, understanding your power relative to each of the other seven tensions affects power dramatically, and knowing how to use these tensions can help you generate counter-power.

CHAPTER 6

Timing Tension

I WANTED TO buy a car for my wife, so I went to the Mercedes dealership. She already had a car, so it was not a rush. I had the luxury of time on my side. I assumed the dealer and salesperson had less of a luxury of time because it was near the end of the month, and I was well aware of monthly quotas and sales being a timing factor. (I recently confirmed this with a sales manager as I bought a car on August 31, 2024. The manager of the dealership was candid with me after I asked how the month had gone. He replied that it had been slow and, as a result, he had more latitude to make a deal.)

After I surveyed the cars inside the showroom, I was approached by a salesperson. I knew I wouldn't find what I was looking for in that room. The showroom is where they put their best vehicles with all the fancy engineering and technology my wife didn't want. However, looking in the showroom whets the appetite of the salespeople because they are looking for a whale—someone who wants the fanciest and, therefore, most expensive car, leading them to the highest commission. I was really a dolphin, not a whale, but I knew how to look like a whale. I stared at the stickers; I asked questions about the latest technologies to get a sense of the salesperson. They were experienced. They were knowledgeable. By asking questions, I learned very quickly who I was negotiating with. This didn't take more than ten to fifteen minutes.

Then I said, "While I like all these features, today I am looking for a simple Mercedes for my wife."

He said, "Okay, let's go to my office."

I respected how fast he pivoted. Again, an experienced salesperson. *No BS*, I thought.

He pulled out several stickers of cars he had on the lot. I looked at one that didn't even have a backup camera—really basic. My wife can back up a trailer; she had already told me that she didn't need and wouldn't use one of those "silly" backup cameras. The sticker for that basic Mercedes was around $40,000. I looked it up in front of him on Kelly Blue Book. It said their price was $33,000 and I should have been able to get it for $35,000. I told him I wouldn't waste his time and would be reasonable. I offered him $33,500. I reasoned that the Mercedes market consisting of conservative bankers who grew up in Nebraska and could back up a trailer was really small, and he would be stuck with that car for a long time. He never asked me about my timing, which was a major mistake. Always know your timing and the timing of the other parties.

The lowest price we got to that day was $37,000. This was after taking several trips to talk to the finance department.

The highest I got that day was $34,500. Once we realized we weren't going to reach a deal, I wished him well and told him that if he ever wanted to sell that car for $34,500, I would buy it. I gave him my card and said, "Call me when you are ready to sell that car to me."

He called me every few weeks to tell me about various sales they were having and how I should come in and see what they had in inventory. I would always ask him whether he still had the car I had looked at, and he would sigh and say, "Yes." This went on for nearly two and a half months. In December of that year, near the end of the year, he called me and said, "Come and get the car. We will do the deal at $34,500." So, I did and gave my wife that car for Christmas.

We don't teach timing, and it is nowhere to be found in *Getting to Yes*. Yet, if you talk to seasoned dealmakers like me, we always say, "Timing is everything." When we discuss, teach, and train negotiation, we focus on the aspects that happen in the room. Yet, as Sun Tzu said, "All battles are won or lost before they are fought." Before you negotiate anything, assess the timing factor. Who does timing favor? Is there any timing tension on either side? You should be able to rate the tension of each side on a scale of one to ten. If you need something today, that is a ten. If you never need it, that is a one. If you could take it or leave it, that is a five. A failure to assess your advantage or disadvantage on timing is disastrous. If you assess it, you can use it to your advantage.

I knew going into the deal that I was a five on timing. Yes, my wife needed a new car, but not today. I knew his timing would revolve around the usual month and year ends. He made a critical mistake in not asking me my timing. If he had, I would have said I was looking for something in the next few months. For the right deal, I would have bought that day, but I didn't have to. I was fine. He thought he had time, but the time he had was affected by the market for that particular car. Nobody else, as near as I could tell, had an interest in that particular car. He should have known that and probably did. Had he known I had months, he would have been more likely to calculate the carry, or in other words, calculate the cost of keeping the car on the lot for a few months. I was the buyer for that unique Mercedes. He treated me like my timing was a ten.

It is important to be aware that timing tension can change over time. On that particular day, we were both at a five on timing. I remained a five. As time went on, he climbed in tension until, by the end of the year, he was at a ten. Timing tension needs to be continually assessed as parties' circumstances change. Constantly assess timing tension and project it forward based on everything else you know.

Is Time a Factor for Any of the Parties?

Deals nowadays are done twenty-four-seven around the clock globally. That wasn't true in 1992 when I was a young lawyer in Chicago at one of the top firms. At the time, the technology for communication was facsimile machines. Wang was the word processor we used, and we thought it a big deal that it could count the words. International travel wasn't as common either. It existed but was expensive and not the go-to method for negotiating an international deal.

In one memorable case, a major international beer producer in Australia had purchased some grain facilities in the Midwest of the US. Grain is integral to beer production, so having lots of sources of grain and being able to hedge that grain in futures markets was essential. The beer producer had decided to sell its US operations to our client, a pure grain operator who, at the time, controlled 25% of the world's grain trade. The beer company's principals and primary lawyers for the US were in Australia, although they also had highly competent lawyers out of Kansas City. We were based out of Chicago.

The proposed transaction structure was a straightforward asset purchase and sale. The primary difference in the work for an asset sale versus a stock sale is that, with a stock sale, all of the assets and liabilities come with the stock. In an asset purchase, you have to state what assets and liabilities you are taking and assuming. Both require extensive due diligence. So, we began to conduct our due diligence from the letter of intent. What assets were we taking? What potential liabilities were associated with them?

In all my books, I emphasize understanding the "why" of a transaction. What is the backstory? What is really going on? I wrote about this deal in *Negotiation as a Martial Art*. I vividly remember going into the kitchen to get a coffee and opening the refrigerator door. It was full of beer. I mean, really full of beer. I recall sharing this with our team, and we learned the following: The two folks this company had sent to the US had apparently partied and lost focus on their hedging. They had lost and were continuing to lose a massive amount of money.

While the Kansas City lawyers were acting calm, cool, and collected, we now knew that every day was hurting the other side. They had timing tension. So, what do you think we did? Let me just say that we conducted the most extensive, time-consuming due diligence I have ever seen. Every dot on every survey had to be explained. Every environmental review we could have performed was performed. We were so extensive that, finally, the other side came to us and said, "What price would you pay for the assets if we close next week?"

We shaved about 25% off the price and closed. The client was thrilled and felt we were geniuses. All we did was find the timing tension and leverage it.

Leverage and Timing Tension

While I segregate these tensions into discrete elements, of course, they play together. Two of the most commonly paired tensions are timing and leverage. In the previous situation, we used timing tension to subtly apply leverage. It worked. But leverage can be used to *create* timing tension. This can be especially powerful when the leverage might shift at a later point. ***Tension Management Point: Be wary that tensions are not static; they are dynamic and can change quickly, especially leverage tension. Always project your tensions over the course of the entire negotiation to avoid surprises.***

Often, external events can change the leverage dynamic. Consider Elon Musk's purchase of Twitter, now X. When he began accumulating shares in January 2022, the world looked very promising. Nasdaq was at 15,000. But then, interest rates began their rapid ascent, and Nasdaq plummeted during that year to as low as 10,000 by December. The world revalued itself, and Musk's powerful bravado early in the year to purchase Twitter with no due diligence quickly turned into a "get me out of this" complete shift in leverage. As we now know, he was forced to complete the transaction, and after litigation, his positions were exposed for being desperate and powerless.

In another case, at one of the universities where I serve on the board of trustees, we were searching for a new dean for one of the schools. I was the representative of the trustees on the search committee. We learned from the search firm that, while we were ahead of the curve, many other prestigious schools were soon to be looking for a dean. We would be in a powerful position until those other searches started building their pool of candidates, and then our power would shift downward. We consciously discussed this timing tension. We set a very aggressive timeline designed to complete our search before other searches were initiated, and as a result, we were able to attract and hire the greatest talent in the market.

Deal and dispute resolution timing can be ruthless. My father contracted prostate cancer at a fairly young age, and he had presented with various symptoms that should have made it obvious that he had that particular cancer. There was a uniform opinion from both the lawyers and the doctors with whom I spoke that he should not have died from it but that the HMO's failure "to timely connect the dots" was the primary reason his cancer was fatal. We hired a top medical malpractice lawyer to review the matter. The potential liability was required to be arbitrated and could not exceed $500,000. Moreover, the medical malpractice lawyer explained to me that the award would be higher if the victim/patient was still alive. What do you think the at-fault HMO did?

The large HMO slow-rolled the case at every turn, which was a successful attempt to use timing to their advantage. My father died, and they quickly settled for about half of the amount my mother would have gotten had he been alive.

Time is money and advantage! A superior negotiator pays close attention to timing tension, both at the beginning and throughout a negotiation. Being able to predict the trajectory of timing tension and the associated power is what makes dealmakers say, "Timing is everything."

CHAPTER 7

Outcome Tension

WHETHER YOU ARE the principal or the agent, whether it is your money or someone else's, the biggest tension in a negotiation is the outcome. All negotiation books and texts focus on getting a better outcome. Outcome-based negotiation is also referred to as *positional bargaining*. You push for an outcome and that is your position. *GTY* was written to propose an alternative to outcome-based negotiation because the authors identified particular evils of positional bargaining. *GTY* says that positional bargaining "produces unwise outcomes," "is inefficient," "endangers an ongoing relationship," and that these negatives become even worse when there are multiple parties. The alternative they posit is *principled negotiation*. You reach principled negotiation by following their four key processes.

The four core principles of *GTY* are 1) to separate the people from the problem, 2) to focus on interests and not positions, 3) to invent options for mutual gain, and 4) to use objective criteria. (There is some variance of opinion on what the key principles of *GTY* are. Sometimes BATNA is included and sometimes not.) All these principles are designed to help with process and outcome tension. That makes sense based on the title *Getting to Yes*. It is about the process of reaching a positive outcome. The outcome is a "Yes" that is acceptable to both parties. But other tensions like who you are dealing with (i.e., relationship), timing, power, intermediaries, and teams are not addressed. Arguably, the first of these—separating the people from the problem—could be used to address some other tension, like relationship. But really, the book is process and outcome-focused. In the *GTY* strategy, you separate the people from the problem not to understand, develop, and use the relationship but to "disentangle" the two so you can apply rational methods to the problem to solve it like a Rubik's Cube. Using objective criteria is a way to justify your position rather than using an agreed-upon process.

While *GTY* has some good fundamental principles, it is too hard on positional bargaining. Rather than avoid outcome tension, great negotiators need to be good at using it both as a sword and a shield. Much of actual negotiation is positional and not susceptible to principled negotiation. Of course, the reality is that when you negotiate and try to use objective criteria as part of your process, it is not as if your counterparty will relent and say, "Thanks for pointing out my error with your objective criteria." On the contrary, they will have their own objective criteria that they will argue are equally valid. You will end up supporting the objective criteria that support your intended outcome.

It isn't that *GTY* is incorrect, but it is overstated because its principled negotiation is only applicable in certain situations. Outcome tension and positional negotiation are applicable in many more scenarios than principled negotiation. To understand outcome tension, it is necessary to understand, compare, and contrast principled negotiation and positional negotiation.

In Defense of Positional Bargaining— Lessons from the Ottoman Empire

The Grand Bazaar in Istanbul, Turkey, is hard to describe if you haven't seen it yourself. For me, it is among the great wonders of the world. As you enter the ancient structure, whose roof has served as a roadway for chase and race scenes for motorcycles in James Bond films, you see endless shops of infinite variety in a maze-like structure. Wide hallways line either side with a variety of stores. Turkish delight shops are like Willy Wonka stores of endless sweets and treats in a variety of colors and flavors. Smiling shopkeepers beckon you into their shops, which vary greatly in size and product type. There are stores with leather goods, gold jewelry, souvenirs, and trinkets, like Turkish coffee cups. There are stores with all types of scarves, purses, and clothing. It's a carousel of delight. The colors are robust and varied, the smell varies with the shops, and there is an underlying energy as peddlers peddle, consumers consume, and hagglers haggle.

My wife wanted some silk scarves for herself and a couple to use as gifts, so we wandered with our tour guide through the never-ending labyrinth. Our guide suggested a store where he knew the owner. Knowing his presence would affect the purity of my impending negotiation experiment, I asked him where it was and asked him to stay behind, which he did. As we approached the small scarf shop, I noticed the owner, who appeared to be forty to fifty years old and had a warm disposition as he engaged with the wandering tourists. We looked in his direction, and he immediately came out into the hall to greet us with a huge smile.

This is, I think, the first myth that we incorrectly teach about positional bargaining. Positional bargaining doesn't mean you are rude, cantankerous, a bully, unreasonable, or anything negative. It just means you are approaching the negotiation with what you want (who doesn't?), and the negotiation is just about one or two factors with little else to discuss. For example, price and quantity (most negotiations are of this type). There may be a future relationship, and understanding that relationship and advancing it will be helpful, but "cooperation" may not be likely to provide a better result. There may be nothing to cooperate on, and forcing some cooperative motif onto the exchange is simply an attempt to alter a clear factual scenario with a framework that doesn't apply.

We shook hands, and all three of us smiled warmly as we entered the scarf shop. The shop owner did not even begin to discuss scarves with us. We sat together as he said, "Let's have some tea. I want you happy. That is what is most important." As I expand on later, almost all bargaining, especially sales, begins with high relationship tension and low outcome tension in the eyes of the buyer. In this scenario, I don't know this person, so I have relationship tension. I don't have a reason to trust this person, and I don't have to buy a scarf (outcome tension). He invites us to sit for tea with him to reduce relationship tension and does nothing to push us to buy a scarf—he doesn't increase our outcome tension. We sit and chat. His English is very good. He asks about our kids and grandchildren. He tells us about his wife and children. He tells us stories; we tell him stories. We laugh, we relax, and he establishes trust as we spend ten to fifteen minutes just visiting. We ask, "What is it like to live in Turkey and in Istanbul? How is the shop's business?" We are as sincerely curious about him as he is about us. It is a genuine attempt to connect at a basic, universal human level.

He then asks what we are looking for and for whom. He begins to pull scarves from the shelf. This is this type of silk; here is another. Feel it; touch it. Which do you like better? "How about colors?" he asks as he pulls more from the shelves. Each time, he watches my wife's face intently. He watches how she touches the scarf and where she touches it. He asks her questions, listens, and adjusts the selections. It's a beautiful exchange to watch as he almost rhythmically works with her feedback. It is like a dance; it has a cadence. When we think of positional bargaining, we don't think of listening attentively and dynamically. We conjure an image of someone who is demanding and recalcitrant and simply wants what they want. But this is not like that. At one point, he wants to show her that this particular fabric she likes can handle water, and he puts on an exhibition with her holding one end and me another and him pouring water on the scarf. The water repels and does not absorb into the soft silk. We are mesmerized.

We select two scarves and ask how much they are. Price had not been mentioned at all up to this point. He works in lira and says he wants the equivalent of $600 for the two scarves. I had done some research, and it was my second time at the Grand Bazaar. The suggestion I was familiar with was to offer half. However, I didn't want to pay more than half. I offered him $100 per scarf or $200. This put our implicit deal—the same as calculating an average—at $400 ($600 + $200)/2, which was more than I wanted to pay. He then offered the implicit deal of $400. I then countered with the implicit deal (the average of his $400 and my $200, which is $300), which he accepted. That was our final deal. You will notice this is half of his original price, and that was not an accident on my part—that was intentional. I will show you how to get to this result, but in simple terms, you need to make an offer that will lead them to split the difference.

There is always an implicit deal halfway between a bid and an ask. I have read the book *Never Split the Difference* several times, and while it is great marketing, splitting the difference is exactly what happens in positional bargaining. It is downright genetic. Splitting the difference is morally justified. The author of *Never Split the Difference* is a hostage negotiator; he is dealing in people. We have known since Solomon that splitting the difference when a human is involved is not possible. But when we are dealing with coins or inanimate things, that is what we do. You and I are in a room. Suppose there is one candy bar. How do we split it? We split it in half. Two parties are married. What do we do in community property states when there is a divorce? We split it in half. Halfway is morally justified. It is, at its core, the "fair share." This is universally true in all countries and cultures.

After we finished our transaction, our host wanted to know if we were happy and if we wanted more tea. I told him I was a teacher and a student of negotiation and asked him if we could sit and chat about his experiences over his twenty-plus years of doing nothing but negotiating every day. He was delighted to chat. I also went and found our tour guide, who he was surprised to see, in case I needed some translation of more sophisticated business terms.

I asked him a simple question: What is the most and the least you have sold a scarf for? His answer was fascinating. The range was between $150 to over $1,000. This was on his most commonly purchased scarf, which he showed me.

I said, "You mean, the very same scarf has sold for as little as $150 and as much as $1,000?"

"Even more than $1,000," he said.

I asked him how he knew where to start to get so much for a scarf. He said he studies the person, especially their clothes and their watch. He said that those wearing a Rolex pay the most. He said they want to pay more because they think the more they pay, the better the product. He said I was dressed casually and wore an Apple Watch, and my wife was dressed plainly, too. I had a Washington University in St. Louis shirt on, and while he didn't know WashU, he decided we were intelligent and practical and that we would buy, but we wouldn't overpay. He had sized us up as pragmatic, no-BS Americans, so he priced the scarf accordingly. Had I been wearing an Armani suit or outfit and a Rolex, I would have paid a lot more for that scarf, he assured me.

Positional bargaining is not bad. People who positional bargain aren't bad. They handle outcome tension with subtle and not-so-subtle human techniques. Positional bargainers can win by playing the halfway game better than their counter-party and using the human techniques that are fundamental to all negotiations, like listening and relationship building. A lot of the outcome in positional bargaining does depend on where you start, called anchoring. But anchoring is contextual and cultural, and if you aren't aware of the context, culture, or message you are sharing, you will overpay for that scarf. The master scarf vendor from Istanbul knew how to build trust and subtly leverage it into an outcome he had predetermined based on his ability to read the outcome the buyer or tourist wanted. He knew how to make each party happy and knew that happiness was subjective!

Reducing Relationship Tension
While Increasing Outcome Tension

The scarf vendor was masterful at removing and preventing tension within me and my wife. We felt initial relationship tension as we entered the shop, of course. But we were greeted with an offer of very good Turkish tea, which we sat and enjoyed. We then talked about families and our lives. We became friends before we ever talked about scarves. By the time we began talking about scarves, he had removed relation-ship tension and established trust. This strong, tension-free relationship led to virtually no process or outcome tension regarding the scarf. Over the years, he had designed a process that minimized process tension and seemed natural and happy. He must have said he wanted us to be happy twenty times during our visit. He made us feel that we could leave at any time, whether we bought a scarf or not, and that we needed to be happy. This was of the utmost importance. If we weren't happy, we shouldn't do it. It was a positional bargain that seemed to celebrate the human element and our uniqueness.

Let's revisit the foundational underpinnings of *Getting to Yes*. Separate the people from the problem. Why? The scarf vendor removed the feeling of any problem. He removed the relationship tension. What was our best alternative to a negotiated agreement? Leaving and not buying a scarf. We could go to another store to buy a scarf, develop lots of scenarios for mutual gain, or use objective criteria to argue for our position. Let's imagine I used these principles. So, after he explained and gave us a price, we could have gone to another scarf store and tried to bid for a lower price based on the competition that exists in the Grand Bazaar. That was certainly a possibility, and I did that for another item where I did not trust the vendor. But we stayed with the scarf vendor because, while he wanted us to buy a scarf, he built a relationship of trust and engaged in a process that made us happy. But as he pointed out, even the very rich customers who wore Rolex watches were happy, too. He met each customer where they wanted to be.

I can't imagine a better sales philosophy, even after forty years of being on every side of thousands of sales. Treat each customer like the unique human that they are. Learn about them, then help them get "where they want to be."

Turkish coffee, if you haven't had it, is really thick and strong. It is nothing like American coffee or European espresso, although it is closer to the latter. To make the thick, rich drink, you need a cezve, a small copper coffee pot. I wanted to buy at least one of these. There were shops in the Grand Bazaar offering these types of wares. I visited one of these shops and asked, "How much for the cezve?" There was no conversation other than the typical haggle. He asked $100, and I offered $5. We ended up at $20, and I looked in the direction of another shop, sending a message that I might just leave.

I visited another shop, and the owner asked for $250, roughly ten times the fair value. I found my tour guide and asked him to ask the owner, "Why so much?" The owner said that he didn't mean anything by it, but I am American, so I should be able to afford it. I didn't buy anything from that store owner even when he tried to reduce the price to $25. No coffee for me and no transaction for him.

Positional bargaining is not good or bad, but it is a reality of negotiation and can be done well or poorly. You can be outcome-driven and still make people happy.

Contexts that Favor Positional Bargaining

While most negotiations have both positional and collaborative elements, some contexts favor positional bargaining and some favor collaborative bargaining. My candy bar example is a perfect example of a context favoring positional bargaining. Let's consider why. In my hypothetical situation, there is only one candy bar and it cannot grow. The quantity is finite. The purchase or sale of a good or service where only quantity and price are the issue are contexts that favor positional bargaining. One of the easiest tests for whether a positional bargaining approach might be appropriate is when you *can* split the difference.

Suppose you are negotiating with a child who is going to prom or some other evening activity. You say, "Be home by midnight." The child says that there is an afterparty that ends at 2 a.m. You can settle on 1 a.m. In another case, suppose you are representing a condo building and negotiating with a developer about how long a restaurant across from your building can be open at night because you are concerned about noise. You want 10 p.m. to be the closing time, and they want midnight. Again, you can split the difference. You may decide not to split the difference, but the negotiation spectrum is linear. Linear spectrum, single-issue negotiations are conducive to positional bargaining. Even in complex negotiations, there can be multiple single-issue matters to be negotiated. Suppose there are two linear spectrum issues related to the restaurant. The first is whether it will resemble a nightclub or family dining, and the second is what role you will have in the approval of the restaurant. You either will or you won't. If it is a family restaurant, you may care less about the hours. If it has the potential to attract a younger crowd, you may forgo the approval as long as it closes at 10 or 11. Negotiation scholars and commentators refer to this as "logrolling."

Complex negotiations may have aspects that are collaborative and aspects that are positional. Positional moves may be made in collaborative negotiations. It is a mistake to think that negotiations are one or the other, value-claiming or value-creating. It isn't that tidy. You will see collaboration attempts in positional scenarios, and positional moves can be very effective at driving collaborative or value-creating activities.

But the important point is that, sometimes, there is a linear problem with no tradeable issue. I have presented a problem to students as well as to highly seasoned negotiators to prove this point. I take two volunteers and ask them to sit across from each other. I then place a $100 bill between them. I tell them to negotiate. Sometimes seasoned negotiators will ask questions of the other like, "Why do you want the bill? Why do you think you deserve the money? What will you spend this money on?" I have had volunteers threaten to just take the hundred-dollar bill. But always, always, always, the two volunteers eventually agree to split the hundred-dollar bill. This is considered "fair." Ask all the questions you want. Probe for underlying motives. When you are done, you are splitting that money.

In conducting this experiment, while the result ended up being an even split, there have been times when it was prolonged and times it was instantaneous. I was guest lecturing in an MBA class and presented two students with the hundred-dollar bill negotiation. Highly competitive and erstwhile negotiation students, they began at 99, 98, etc. Based on their behavior, I think their peer spectators placed great pressure on them to win. It took them forever. The fastest I have seen it done is in one of my law school classes. As soon as I put the bill down, the two of them almost simultaneously said, "Let's split it."

Contexts Favoring Collaborative Bargaining (aka Value-Sharing)

Collaborative bargaining is described as value-creating. You don't split what is available; the context allows you to achieve results that are not obvious from the initial claims. This is accomplished through examining differences by asking questions and probing for diverse needs and wants. There are multiple issues, and one party might care more about one than the other. Trades are made based on a better understanding of the other party's needs and wants.

I have been the president of the HOA at a luxury condo residence in Austin since 2013. It's a high-rise next to a luxury-affiliated hotel. A developer decided to buy the land across the street from our condo building to build a hotel of about equivalent height. Residents of urban high-rises have some immediate tensions when these situations arise. You can feel the tension the minute that the possibility of a neighboring building arises. It begins with emails, text messages, and phone calls. At the next HOA board meeting, it will be on the agenda. Why? Neighboring building developments might affect views and view corridors. I used to be able to see some landmark or attractive element of the city, and now I can't. There might now be people in the new building who can see into my unit. There might be lights on the new building affecting my peace and quiet. There might be noise from a bar or late-night restaurant that is part of the building. There will be a construction period with associated impacts on traffic, and it will generate noise and dust. Segment the tensions, and you will find:

- Relationship Tension: The counterparty is a real estate developer who has conveniently donated to every campaign of every city council member and appears to be best friends with the mayor.
- Process Tension: They don't have to sit with you. They don't have to meet with you. They don't have to deal with you as long as they don't need any type of zoning exception or other approval.
- Timing Tension: They have every incentive to start as quickly as possible and continue until they are done. For a developer, time is money. So, all the timing pressure is on the resident building and its constituents.
- Leverage Tension: They hold all the power. They don't need us, and we cannot object to the building. A good developer always seems to have the city in their pocket even if there is an objectionable issue. That is not necessarily evil or wrong in any respect. The city, especially when it comes to the central business district, has a substantial interest in turning an empty lot into a taxpayer and positive element.
- Outcome Tension: Residents quickly imagine a world where they lose everything and their condo home declines in value. Traffic resulting from the new building and residents and/or hotel guests driving in and out will make

the ingress and egress of their building impossible. The view of the capital is gone. Construction is untenable to live next to. They will be miserable for two years while streets are blocked, cement pours light up the night, and construction noise requires all to wear earplugs. The new first-floor bar will keep them up at night. The new sign will shine right in their window.

As you can see, five core tensions are already in full bloom.

I trust it is clear that this is very different than putting a candy bar or $100 bill between two volunteers.

Positional Tension – Tug of War

The biggest fear of positional bargaining is that it will result in a stalemate, a tug of war. It certainly starts that way and can stay that way if you don't understand and use the seven tensions. A tug of war implies that the sole focus is the outcome. You need to use the other tensions to break that stalemate. *GTY* offers you process-outcome tension solutions to outcome tension clashes. Ignoring who is on the other side of the tug-of-war rope won't help you; endearing the person on the other side of the rope will. A general principle of focusing on interests and not positions and inventing options for mutual gain won't help you if there is one candy bar and each side wants it. We can't dismiss positional bargaining; we need a framework to do it well.

Positional Bargaining and its Role in Driving Collaboration

When you talk to tough positional bargainers (the type that people think of when they criticize all positional bargaining), they will tell you exactly why they come in strong with demands. Not one of them will tell you they think they are being mean or unreasonable. My toughest positional negotiating friends and counterparties will say things like, "It helps get the other side focused."

Outcome tension can be divided into various sub-tensions related to the other tensions. Some of those are:

1. Getting less than what you want (power tension)
2. Getting less than you could have (power tension)
3. Upsetting your counterparty(ies) (relationship tension)
4. Getting a bad reputation (relationship tension)
5. Suboptimal outcome due to being too late or too early (timing tension)
6. Suboptimal outcome because your agent was inadequate or talked you into it (agency tension)
7. Suboptimal outcome due to team dysfunction (team tension)

The classic negotiation tension arises from worrying about getting less than we want or not getting what we want at all. I want a candy bar. I want a car. I want a house. If I don't get what I want, I will be unhappy. One of the classic definitions of unhappiness is being unsatisfied, i.e., not achieving the outcome we desired.

Outcome tension is very palpable and often leads to outcome fear. Negotiators are often afraid of leaving money on the table. What if there was more available and you didn't get it? On a related basis, some negotiators are afraid of being labeled a "sucker." Some fear being too aggressive or not aggressive enough regarding the outcome. Some fear a risk to the relationship and compromise their result in favor of the relationship. Some folks are pleasers and while not afraid, per se, they want to ensure happiness at the end.

The Fear of Leaving Money on the Table

Mostly, this fear arises because we don't know what could have happened in a negotiation because we never deal with that person again in the same context to find out "how we did." But in active markets, you can get a very real read on your outcome. One of my investment strategies is buying and selling luxury condos from high-end brands like The Four Seasons, The Ritz, Auberge, and Montage. I have engaged in over twenty-five luxury condominium transactions. In these markets, I can get a quick report card on my purchases because I sell most of them after one or two years. On the selling side, it can be more difficult to know how I did because the property must "re-trade" and sell again for comparison. Generally, I have done very well. However, I've made two sales that clearly left money on the table. In both cases, a fairly short time after I sold the units, they re-traded for substantially more, indicating I could have gotten more when I sold them. While I was initially disappointed in the transactions, after analysis, I understood why it happened.

In both cases, I had timing tension. I had something else I wanted to buy with that capital that I thought was a better return opportunity.

Nevertheless, I could have gotten more than I did. After using my tension analysis, my timing tension overrode my outcome tension. But I didn't calculate it. I should have compared the maximum I could have made on the deal with the extra return I would get from redeploying the capital. I needed to rebalance that in the future.

The tension analysis showed me an opportunity for improvement in my negotiation strategy. Between the two deals, I probably left $500,000 on the table. Was the timing such that I made an extra $500,000 because I moved more quickly on the subsequent deals? Maybe I need more slack in my general capital so I can be more patient? Considering the tensions I faced, I can now calculate the cost of the extra capital and the necessity of timing on the future transactions to make sure what I am doing is financially intelligent. ***Tension Management Point: Use an analysis of your tensions in order to improve your negotiation skills. Understand "why" you favor one tension over another and make sure it is financially intelligent and justifiable.***

The Fear of Hurting Others' Feelings

Different personalities have different tensions when it comes to negotiating. Some negotiators are concerned about hurting someone else. This is usually a form of relationship tension. You either have or will experience a relationship with someone you don't want to hurt over some object or objective. It could also be the nature of the negotiator themself. Some negotiators are just too timid. While this can be improved through training, it supports using agent tension and team tension. If you worry too much about how people feel about you, you need to hire an agent to handle your negotiations and/or, if circumstances allow, use the benefits of a team with various types of negotiators on it. The key is to know this about yourself.

The Fear of Being a Sucker (Reputational Fear)

This is the most common fear of normal folks. What if I don't get what I should? What if I miss something big? This is especially true of early-stage negotiators. It is not an irrational concern. The best way to battle this fear is with the help of agents, subject matter experts, or a team. If none of those are available to you, then you need to do some research on outcomes.

You would be amazed at the data available to you through your contacts and internet searches that can help guide you regarding values. It is not that those data points provide you with all the answers, but they can help you prepare to address information that is available to your constituents or client in case they do a search or make an inquiry of their subject matter experts.

An employee sued our large staffing company for disability discrimination in South Carolina. When I reviewed the case with our general counsel, it looked like our client and our team had done all we could to accommodate the employee's disability once we were given notice of the disability. Our lawyers weren't quite sure how big the exposure could be. They could calculate the cost of litigation but had some trouble figuring out what it would mean if we lost. Now, they don't teach you this in law school, but I googled "Average settlement in a disability discrimination case in South Carolina." Of course, that is not necessarily the answer, but it is a data point. If you are unsure, get yourself some data. If the lawyers came to me with a settlement of $50,000, I would at least have the ability to compare their number to this data point, how it was different than other cases, and other critical analyses. The point is, to reduce your fear of getting less than what you should, do some research to find support for what is normal in a particular situation. This is a good opportunity to use the *GTY* principle of an objective standard.

The Fear of Being a Jerk (Reputational Fear II)

This is a less common fear. Most jerks aren't afraid of being jerks; that is part of what makes them jerks. But there are lots of jerks who just have an inadequate or inaccurate view of themselves and don't want to be thought of as a jerk. This fear is different than the fear of hurting others' feelings in that the fear itself is of developing a reputation in the community that nobody wants to deal with, and if they have to deal with you, you will be presumed to be someone with whom you have to be incredibly aggressive leading to suboptimal outcomes for your clients.

The Fear of Killing the Deal

This fear is unique to agents like attorneys. The agents have to walk a delicate balance between getting everything they should (avoiding sucker syndrome) and pushing so hard there is no deal (fear of killing the deal). This is the boogeyman of agents representing principals.

The Interplay with the Other Tensions

There is no better strategy for outcome tension than passing it back to the other party. If you have to have something and there is no option other than you getting it, then will have a hard time negotiating. At that point, you are begging, not negotiating. As Sun Tzu said, "All battles are won or lost before they are fought." You have already lost if you have to have it. You will overpay.

I saw this as a young deal lawyer at a major corporation. A major executive had his sights on a major acquisition target. No matter the price, he modified the justification so that it still worked. The deal was a disaster and, ultimately, sold at a loss. Most of us have been there ourselves. Strategy or necessity overtakes rational evaluation. As I said earlier, when it comes to selling a business, my savvy friends say, "If you have one buyer, you have no buyer." So much of negotiation is about choice. If you have no choice, you will have a hard time negotiating. You have the ultimate outcome tension.

But assuming you have the choice of buying or not buying, selling or not selling, settling or not settling, you need to pay attention to outcome tension. When you feel that tension, you need to assess the other tensions and see which ones you can use to hand tension back to the other side. To do that, you must be comfortable with a "no deal" scenario.

I gave an example of this in international strategy. When Putin put his troops on the border of Ukraine, the US and Europe froze. Had we mobilized, then Putin would have had a hard decision to make. That would have flipped the script.

In the car dealership example, you have the ability to avoid the traps of the other tensions and keep yourself from being walked down the rabbit hole. You don't have to play their game. You don't have to sit in their office. You don't have to wait while they go back and forth. You don't have to buy that day.

I was negotiating an employment dispute for a client. (For purposes of confidentiality, all of the amounts are fictitious approximations.) Virtually all of these cases settle for two simple reasons: legal expenses and uncertain outcomes. For a plaintiff's lawyer, they are generally on a contingency fee. They will collect some portion of any recovery, including a settlement. If they take the case to trial and lose, they get nothing. The defendant will face escalating legal expenses and soft costs, such as the distraction of involved witnesses and the uncertainty of outcome.

In this case, the plaintiff's demand was $300,000. The BATNA for the defendant was more like $100,000. As I got closer to $100,000, they were still in the range of $250,000. I didn't want to ship the case off to a litigator, so I felt high outcome tension. I went to my client and said, "I can justify

$100,000, but no more. If you can support that, I am going to end the negotiation and let them make the hard decision." He said he agreed. I told him to prepare a check. I sent the plaintiff's counsel a picture of the check and said, "This is all I got." I told him if they wanted it, they could have it, but otherwise, we were done.

He wrote me emails. He tried to split the difference. He tried to argue more facts with me. I didn't respond except to reiterate the deal we would do. Eventually, they accepted the deal.

In another case, I was negotiating a commercial dispute between one of my clients and a major bank. I was dealing with a subsidiary of the bank. They wouldn't go above $100,000, and my client wanted a minimum of $250,000. At the last minute, they came to $125,000, and I indicated a willingness to accept $200,000. When it deadlocked, I wrote the counterparty and said we would be proceeding with arbitration. We prepared the arbitration papers, and I reached back out to the counterparty, who was a lawyer. I simply asked him to whom I should send the arbitration. He gave me the name of a litigation lawyer at their parent company headquarters. I sent them the arbitration. The litigation lawyer wrote me, saying, "You know, you weren't that far apart in the negotiation. Maybe we should try that again." We negotiated for an amount that my client considered acceptable.

In all these situations, I took the stress of deciding whether to settle and gave it to the other side. Confidence in your alternative will make you a better positional negotiator.

Relationship Tension – The People and the Problem

People and problems are always intertwined, and that is why I object to the negotiating principle "separate the people from the problem." If your child wants to go to a prom afterparty and you don't want them to go out of concern for their safety, the problem and the person are inextricable. You are not worried about the prom afterparty; you are worried about this child, your child, going to that party. If your child tries to separate the people from the problem or deploy objective standards, they might say, "All the other parents are letting their kids go." If it is true, and it might be, that is an objective standard. Of course, you will reject that immediately. When I said something like that, my parents would always retort, "If everyone else jumped off a bridge, would you?" You will still say no, and you will say you don't care what the other parents are willing to do. No means no. You might compromise a 2 a.m. curfew to a 12 a.m. or 1 a.m.—but not because you are looking for a win-win scenario. You are trying to parent and, therefore, preserve the relationship and achieve an acceptable outcome.

Emotions are a reality of many, if not most, negotiations because the underlying subject matter is packed with emotion. Suppose you are negotiating to buy a house or car. These are emotional purchases because you are going to live in that house and you are going to live in that car. You imagine yourself in the car. You imagine yourself living in the house. Before buying these items, you drive the car and spend time in the house. The more time you spend in that car and in that house, the greater likelihood you will buy it.

If I am selling the house or the car, I want to do the opposite of separating the people from the problem. I want you to feel like you must have it. I want you happy in that house or car. Like my friend from Istanbul, the product becomes secondary to how you feel, so I want you to feel good. As he said to us, "I want you happy."

Positional bargainers reel you in, and that is a skill you need. The idea of deconstructing emotions and isolating negotiating principles on an intellectual basis might work in a classroom but not with humans.

CHAPTER 8

Team Tension

VIRTUALLY EVERY NEGOTIATION involves other constituents on your side, if not a team. Once you are part of a team of negotiators, you are in a multi-party negotiation with your own side. I will focus both on what to do with your own team and how to deal with your opponent's team.

We are drawn to people who think like we do (known as the Similar to Me Effect). When we hire and build a team, we tend to pick people like us. This is a mistake. Cloning syndrome is a real problem and one that is hard to recognize. I remember when the Union Pacific Railroad sent me to leadership school as a young, budding manager soon to take over responsibility of the railroad's airfreight division. We were sent a battery of psychological tests to complete before the "school" began. In one of the early days, they split us into teams to solve a problem. I remember thinking I had drawn the lucky straw because I liked all my teammates. They were all extroverted, intuitive, thinking types that saw possibilities.

They were bright and articulate. I couldn't wait. Sure enough, in very short order, we completed the task with plenty of time to spare. We high-fived and patted each other on the backs. It was easy and fun, and we got a good score.

They then gave us a new team for a slightly different task. I didn't know or recognize the people in this group. They were a mix of folks I hadn't spent much time with. Some were introverts who I hadn't heard contribute anything. We began the task. It was slow going. The team couldn't agree, and we seemed to fight about everything. Every single issue was work and required compromise. It was unpleasant. When we finished, there were no high fives, no pats on the back. Then, we were scored on our results. This heterogeneous group way outscored our homogeneous group. I was stunned but learned an important lesson. Diversity leads to better results.

I am a very straightforward, rational, and transparent negotiator. That is my style. I function well with a client or teammate who is tough and unreasonable. The black hat, white hat team, according to studies, is a very successful team. I have witnessed this in my own negotiations. If you are on the unreasonable, strong, and demanding side, find yourself someone who is reasonable and compromises.

I tend to pair perfectly with extremely demanding clients. I once represented the CEO of a large public utility in Texas. He had taken the company public, and then it was taken private by a large private equity firm. The private equity firm decided they didn't need him. He could tell it was coming before they told him, and he immediately reached out to me for guidance on how to handle the large PE firm.

This guy was tough. He had set a record for the most broken helmets on his rural Texas high school football team. He was fearless, an outcome-driven negotiator, and relatively uncompromising. But he knew those traits would not get him what he wanted. He and I were a great black hat, white hat team.

Since my client's president had just been fired, my client figured he was next. Instead of waiting for a letter of termination, I preemptively wrote them in a friendly tone and conveyed that we knew they wanted him to move on, so we should engage in some conversations to see if we could work out a mutually agreeable solution. They did not expect this communication. We engaged in a series of communications to see how far apart our expectations of his entitlements were under his various contracts with them. We were very far apart.

In the midst of these early conversations, the law firm sent a check to my client via FedEx for a seven-figure amount, but it was still substantially less than what we thought he was owed. My client called me while furiously screaming at the FedEx delivery person. The note just said, "Enclosed please find a check in full and final settlement of the dispute." On the back, it had a restrictive endorsement that made it clear that accepting this check was a full satisfaction of the claim. I was stunned. A major New York law firm was communicating directly with my client without including me. Now, I was incensed as well. I told my client that I would complain to the lawyers, but he had to contact the client PE firm. And he did. It must have been quite the performance because the lawyers called me before I could call them and said, "We think your client is crazy." To which I responded, "I think you may be right. I have never quite seen him like this before, and I have known him for over ten years."

Note that this was a positional bargaining move of the worst type. (As I mentioned earlier, I have used a similar tactic but at the end of a negotiation, not the beginning.) No "hello," no tea, no building of a relationship. I hadn't had any substantive conversations with the NY counsel, let alone any time to build trust. When the PE firm learned what had happened from my "crazy" client, their managing director, who was also a lawyer, contacted me and said I wouldn't have to deal with the NYC lawyers again. I would deal directly with him. There were two more times when my client acted crazy, and between my calm, cool, rational approach and his craziness, we ended up with seven times the amount originally sent by FedEx. It was a beautiful team of a black hat and a white hat. Build your team with diversity in every dimension you can. This includes gender, race, culture, ethnicity, national origin, and other general diversity measures.

In a class I teach, we put together teams to attempt to negotiate an international joint venture. One year, the students asked if they could assemble their own teams. I hadn't allowed this before, but I thought I would give it a try. It was a disaster. Students from the same country formed teams. Students who were friends formed teams. They were all driven to (unintentionally) build the original type of team I was on in leadership school where there were no differences. They were driven by the cloning effect. Cloning is fun and self-fulfilling. The teams' results were suboptimal. When the teams negotiated, they treated each other poorly, on some occasions laughing at their differences. It was hard to watch. I knew I had made a big mistake. I had eliminated healthy team tension and really ruined "who was in the room."

Not only did I never do that again, I redoubled my efforts to create diverse teams. If there were six teams and I had six students from Italy, I would make sure there was one on each team. If I felt like there were six strong leaders, I separated them. Every class or category I could identify was spread around intentionally. That has proved a winning strategy in every subsequent class.

Besides diversity of thought, opinion, and style, you need to make sure you have all the subject matter experts (SME) you need. If you are negotiating over real estate, you need people who understand that market and understand real estate. You may accomplish this through an agent. If you are negotiating for the purchase of staffing services, you need someone on your team who understands staffing services of the type you are purchasing. If you are outsourcing aerospace engineering services, you need engineering types on your team. You want to ensure you don't have a blind spot.

When building a negotiation team, you also want some representatives from any users who will be impacted by the purchase. If you are buying copy machines, you should have someone from the administrative group and the primary users of the equipment.

In summary, to build a team, you need diverse methods and styles, people who know the subject matter, and representatives of the user community. You should think in broad terms about the community within which your "team" operates because the team will represent the culture and reflect other traits of the community.

The team is always smaller than the community, and some members of the community are less present than others. Some community members are downright invisible. When we think of a team, we think of players on a field or court. Sometimes, basketball is thought of as akin to business. Anyone can score, dribble, handoff, and assist, but no one player can do it all. When they do, they only get so far. The Mavericks couldn't win with just Luka Doncic, no matter how good he is. Michael Jordan needed Scottie Pippen, Steve Kerr, John Paxton, Dennis Rodman, and many other teammates. Stars are stars of a team. They may have the most points, but the great ones also have the most assists. Sometimes, they are injured. Sometimes, they are sick. Sometimes, they foul out. A team with only one star is a good team but rises and falls solely by the star and cannot achieve sustained greatness.

When we see the five-player "team" on the court, who is behind that? Yes, there is a bench. In fact, in basketball, there are six players on the bench. So, now we have eleven players on the "team." Who directs them? The captain, somewhat, but there is also a head coach and assistant coaches. I have floor seats for the Dallas Mavericks right behind the team's bench. You would be amazed by how many people congregate around that bench. There are former players or injured players, friends of the players, and owners and their assistants lurking nearby or in a suite. And, of course, there are trainers, nutritionists, strength and conditioning folks, and analysts who study the games and video them to improve performance. Of course, you need scouts to find the next group of players and medical staff to take care of the ones you have. Then, you have marketing folks, broadcasting people, and the usual array of operations staff doing things like payroll. When you are done looking at the five on the floor and considering the real community on the other side, you are now in the one hundred to two hundred range of community members. Yet, you watch a handful of the community. You don't see 90% of the total team, which is the community. Make sure you understand your team and your counterparty's team in the broadest sense.

When you deal with teams and communities, it is critical that you know the roles of each individual on the team. If they don't tell you their roles, you need to ensure you do your research thoroughly. You don't want to talk to a user the same way you would talk to a procurement representative. They have very different "love languages."

I was president for many years of one of the largest aerospace and defense staffing firms in the US. Boeing was our biggest client, but we did business with every major aerospace and defense company, providing, in many cases, classified engineers to design the next generation of aircraft, missiles, and other weapons. The procurement of our services was done through RFPs, requests for proposals. There would be an informational round and then a price competitive round or multiple rounds. The best buyers of our services had very diverse and sometimes large teams of individuals. They were ad hoc committees or task forces put together for the special purpose of buying these services. These teams had all the diversity I described. They would be from different units of the enterprise, and they would be from different geographies. They would have financial analysts, subject matter experts, and members who understood staffing services and outsourcing. Their culture would reflect the culture of the larger community.

To be a great negotiator on either side of the table, you need to understand the roles, culture, style, and decision-making process of the team. All of the advice I outlined around building a relationship with an individual now comes into play regarding an organization.

CHAPTER 9

Agent Tension

MANY NEGOTIATIONS INVOLVE agents, including representatives such as real estate brokers, accountants, and lawyers. There are various sub-tensions when you retain an agent and other sub-tensions when you are an agent. This chapter will discuss agent tension in connection with the other tensions and sub-tensions.

How do you know when you need an agent? This could be the subject of a book itself. In simple terms, agents are retained for several reasons, including:

1. The agent has special expertise that you don't have. If you are negotiating with the IRS, you will need a tax accountant or a tax lawyer.

2. The agent has access to resources that you don't have. While you can do a real estate transaction without a broker, they have access to forms of contracts and relationships with title companies, photographers, and stagers.

3. The agent has focus, dedication, and time you don't have. A negotiation is often a one-off for the average person. A professional does these types of negotiations for a living.
4. It is required by law or regulation, meaning you need a license to engage in certain activities.
5. It is required by industry practice. For example, insurers often only distribute their insurance products through a broker.

Retaining an Agent

There should be a contract detailing the relationship between you and the agent. For a real estate broker, there will be a form of broker agreement that is most likely sanctioned by the local Realtor association. Be assured that, regardless of what the agent tells you, all agency fees are negotiable. Please note that in a 2023 settlement, real estate companies basically admitted they were colluding on commission pricing of 6%, and the entire business is being rethought and repriced as a result of a major lawsuit. If your agent won't negotiate fees, interview a few others. **Negotiation Tip: having more choices leads to better results.** You should set expectations regarding the representation so you can evaluate the performance of the representative. Consider your expectations for the other tensions: outcome, relationship, time, process, power, and team. You should have a written plan with your agent to ensure you are aligned on the seven tensions, including their agency. In a simple real estate transaction, it might be like this:

I want to get at least $750,000 for my real estate (outcome tension). I don't plan on having an ongoing relationship with the buyer (relationship tension). I want the property sold in ninety days (timing tension). I want to be updated weekly or about significant events (agency tension) and given two days' notice of showings (process tension). Otherwise, I am leaving the process to the agent. I want to negotiate from a position of strength because if I can't sell it for the amount I want in ninety days, I will just rent it (power tension). Having my agent aligned with my tensions will increase the likelihood of successful representation.

Managing the Agent

Agents are generally not well managed because the seven tension expectations are not explicitly set out in advance of the representation. If you take the time to document these tensions, managing the agent becomes as easy as using a tension expectation template. See Appendix E for a template on the seven tensions to get you and your agent on the same page.

What If You Are the Agent?

If you are the agent, you should want the very same template the client wants. You will want to be as clear as possible about what you can and cannot do. You will want your client to have a reasonable outcome goal. You will want your client to have a reasonable timing goal. You will want to be as clear as possible on the plan for how you will engage with the other side.

Although I am a lawyer, one of my early encounters using another lawyer in a matter was instructive of how we should act. He said, "I will treat your money as if it were mine." I knew he wasn't saying he would steal from me; he meant I would get his best. I would get the highest level of diligence and attention. And I did.

Each year in my class, I give students some actual employment cases for negotiating settlements. They tend to be discrimination or wrongful termination cases. They don't know which side they will represent, so they have to prepare both sides. This is important so they can see each side's viewpoint and can assist in an agreeable resolution. As part of settling such a case, they have to brainstorm potential offers in the form of "goodies" for the employee besides just money. For example, ongoing health or retirement benefits. The key to negotiating these cases is having lots of potential items of value at your disposal because different plaintiff employees may be attracted to different things. I ask the students, who prepare for this negotiation with co-counsel in teams, to brainstorm as many items as possible. They tend to generate three to four items.

I originally figured they only had three or four items because, at this stage of their life, they didn't know as much about employment. But then I ran an experiment. I started putting them into teams and giving them the following assignment: Suppose you were hired by a law firm and the only item you agreed on was salary. What else might you ask for in your negotiation with your new employer?

I give them twenty minutes and make it a contest to make it interesting. The winning team always generates over one hundred ideas, including items like bring your dog to work day, remote work capability, unlimited vacation time, and many other creative ideas. When they are done and celebrating and high-fiving each other, I ask a simple question: What should I tell their client from last week about the fact that they could generate over one hundred ideas for themselves but only three or four for their client? I let that question sit for a bit.

The point of the exercise is clear. You should be like that early lawyer I used. Put the same level of effort, diligence, creativity, and passion into your client's matter as you would your own. This is a lesson to live by if you are an agent.

Precautions for Agent: Confidentiality, Conflicts, and Collegiality

Confidentiality. Agents are supposed to maintain confidentiality, and I think most do so. I think their primary obligation, as they perceive it, is to keep the information confidential from the public, strangers, and those not involved with the transaction or dispute. However, I have noticed that some agents use confidential information to gain an advantage in a negotiation. For example, suppose I tell a real estate agent I will not pay over $1,000,000 for a piece of real estate. And suppose I specifically tell the agent not to disclose my highest price. I don't want the seller to know my best and final offer because I might want to say it is $950,000. Unfortunately, I have had agents who have disclosed that I might go to a million. I think agents sometimes think this is an okay way to proceed, but for me, it is not okay unless I consent to it.

To understand this, consider that the agent is confusing two of the seven tensions. They are thinking that I am only trying to dictate an outcome. However, I am actually trying to dictate the process. I don't want them to know my bottom line because it has to do with how I want the negotiation to proceed. Therefore, if you are using an agent, be as clear as you can about the use of your confidential data, even as a tactic. And if you are an agent, it is important that you get your principal's or client's permission before you disclose information, even if you think it is tactically smart or helpful.

Conflicts. There are formal conflicts, and there are informal conflicts. Most formal conflicts are well managed and cared for, but there are a lot of informal conflicts or conflicts around the edges. A formal conflict is the representation of two parties whose interests conflict, like representing the buyer and seller on a transaction or representing two parties getting a divorce. Although, with certain waivers, a client can agree to these types of formal conflicts, it is simply improper without consent.

However, there are more subtle informal conflicts. These are often familial or friendship-oriented. Suppose I am buying property, and my real estate agent is married to a lawyer who is representing the seller. Or suppose my banking lawyer is married to a broker who routinely represents the landlord from whom I am leasing space. Even in larger cities, the number of professionals is small, and I am amazed at some of the coincidental relationships. This is another reason why understanding who you are dealing with and what their relationships are with others is absolutely a critical part of your due diligence and negotiation.

Collegiality. This precaution considers relationships between agents on opposite sides. It is not unusual for agents to deal with each other more often than they deal with you. This is a form of informal conflict because they could use your outcome as one of a series of conflict outcomes with the opposing agent. For example, suppose you are a lawyer who regularly represents plaintiffs against another lawyer who regularly represents companies. The relationship with your "opposing" counsel may be such that you are caught up in a pattern of results as opposed to being truly the stand-alone outcome you want.

I was recently involved in a hiring process. I have been involved in hundreds of hiring processes and have been in the talent acquisition business for more than twenty-five years. In this case, we had to select a search firm. Some members of the team, who regularly retained search firms, avoided a top firm as a candidate and were pushing what I (and probably others) considered a lesser firm. I used one of my favorite words and said, "Why? Why ABC Associates?" The team members explained that this firm was good but always came in second in their search firm selection process. We interviewed several firms, and ABC Associates was not the best, although they were fine. I pushed and asked, "Why wouldn't we select the best?" They said they felt sorry for this firm for always missing out but being close.

Their job to do what was best was being impacted by their role in the search community. I completely understand and understood those feelings. But this search deserved the best, and I was pretty firm that we shouldn't retain them based on the relationship that had developed. We selected the best, and we ended up hiring the best candidate.

In another case, I worked with a real estate agent with a special niche within a designated cultural subgroup. I thought she was a strong agent and would represent me well. However, as she brought buyers, she only brought buyers from her cultural subgroup, and very quickly, it was no longer about me and her duties to me.

These are soft conflicts of interest. They don't cause a direct conflict, but loyalty can be impacted by cultural, societal, and professional bonds. I try to be aware of this when I am an agent and when I hire an agent. If you are an agent, be honest about the potential for conflicts, even outside of what your profession regulates. If you are hiring an agent, do not be afraid to do your diligence to make sure you know all the hard and soft conflicts that might exist.

Agents are a reality of deals and dispute resolution. I know some people who believe anyone who negotiates their own deals is a fool. However, it is critically important that, whether you are the agent or the client, you have a written agreement stipulating expectations on all of the seven tensions. As an agent, be open and honest about any and all potential issues that may arise and any potential threats to confidentiality or your professional judgment. As a client, do not be shy. You are entitled to do your due diligence with respect to your potential agent. If you encounter resistance, you should presume that there is an issue.

CHAPTER 10

What is Collaboration in a Negotiation Context?

POSITIONAL BARGAINING IS often decried as non-collaborative, and collaboration is considered the highest form of negotiation. Have you ever been told to collaborate? Have you ever heard that negotiation is more successful if we aren't competitive but rather collaborative? Aren't we supposed to find "win-win" solutions through collaboration? When we manage an organization, do we not ask, if not demand, that our associates collaborate? The answer to all these questions is YES! We expect people to collaborate, and by that, we most simply mean to work together.

Wonderful! And yet, have any of us taught others how to collaborate and work well together? Did anyone teach us how to collaborate? For the most part, the answer to these questions is a resounding NO!

As a practitioner, student, and teacher of negotiation, I have read plenty of negotiation books about collaborative problem-solving in lieu of fighting when it comes to reaching an agreement. How do we do that? As you will see, all the same issues you face when you negotiate come to bear when you attempt to collaborate.

Lessons from *Gilligan's Island*

A research professor and expert scoutmaster, an experienced boat captain and his young and eager first mate, a billionaire, a socialite, a movie star, and a young general store employee from Kansas find themselves in a predicament. They are stranded on an uncharted island and want to escape. The billionaire needs to pay attention to his stocks. The movie star is still in her gown from the night before and needs to get in touch with her agent. The professor can create and build anything out of organic materials. They have a working radio, a gun, and a flare gun. The boat captain exercises leadership skills and encourages collaboration. The young lady from Kansas is practical and no-nonsense. The range of talents is impressive and broad. And yet, after ninety-nine episodes spanning three years, they remained on the island. Getting off the island required successful collaboration, but that didn't happen. Successful collaboration requires more than talent, leadership, technical expertise, technology, and a shared goal.

What kept that team on the island for three years and ninety-nine episodes? Some of my most enjoyable research for this book was to rewatch many of the episodes of

Gilligan's Island, which ran from 1964-1967. What were the impediments to collaboration success? The answer is one articulate, very well-intentioned, bumbling teammate who derailed many of the team's efforts. Gilligan knocked down huts, destroyed rafts, ate materials the professor made for other purposes, and had endless moments that dashed potential escape or rescue plans. It really was Gilligan's Island. Are you surprised a single dysfunctional team member can derail the entire team?

Who is "the team"? We often consider the team to be the small group that is acting or playing. A basketball team is often considered to be the five folks on the floor. But "the team" is almost always a broader group that includes those who aren't in the room—and there are many more of them. They form what I call the "negotiation community." Similarly, on Gilligan's Island, the team that is collaborating includes Skipper, Gilligan, Thurston Howell III and his wife (Lovey), Ginger, Professor, and MaryAnne. However, there are team members who want to keep the characters on the island. Senior management (in the form of producers and writers) don't really want to see the island team succeed because they will be out of a job. Senior management is more interested in perpetuating their jobs than in succeeding. Anyone who has ever worked in a large company may recognize that fact pattern.

But there is much more at work here. As the characters develop, their backstories emerge. We learn by episode four that Skipper has PTSD from World War II. Eager to get Skipper to relive his war experience on Guadalcanal so he can remember how he once turned a radio into a transmitter, the other team members give him a dose of tranquilizers to make him reconnect with that previous experience. Unfortunately, because he is in a semi-hypnotic state, they miss a chance to communicate with a plane flying overhead. Well-intentioned overzealousness was an enemy of their collaboration.

By episode five, after many failures to escape the island, leadership becomes an issue as the billionaire challenges the skipper for control. Professor runs an election for President of the Island, creating a voting booth and official ballots. The billionaire tries to buy the vote, offering the Kansas store clerk a job for $50,000 a year and telling Ginger he will buy Hollywood. He offers Gilligan the job of Secretary of the Navy. Skipper encourages the team not to change the skipper mid-ocean. However, the winner of the presidency after several recounts is Gilligan, who won on a write-in basis. The most incompetent team member was elevated to lead the team to keep leadership out of the hands of the two antagonists. The two antagonists anoint themselves as Vice President and Chief Justice, and everyone gets a major job. Since they are all too busy with their own "portfolios," the administration, under the threat of impeachment, dissolves and fails.

These scenarios and situations resonate with our experiences working with each other. The sitcom *Gilligan's Island* reflects serious business scenarios I have seen in nearly forty years of personal business and legal activity. The issues are universal, as is obvious from the fact that this was all written in the middle of the twentieth century. Yet, the sitcom is as popular as ever. If diversity of talent, common goals, enthusiasm, focus on team leadership, coordination, and all those success factors you read about in academic literature don't lead to success, what does?

Collaboration is one of those soft skills like listening that gets scant attention, and yet, we are supposed to collaborate with our counterparties to succeed in negotiations. If we don't collaborate well, we are disadvantaged. Negotiation literature teaches us that we need to be collaborative and not competitive. What does that even mean? Competitiveness is easily understood and recognized. Two of us want the same candy bar, and I want to get as much of it as I can, regardless of what you want or get. How can two people collaborate over the candy bar?

Collaboration as a Process

Telling people to collaborate is unhelpful because collaboration is the result of other human activities. I don't automatically want to collaborate with you because I don't know you and I don't trust you. There are important predicates to a desire or willingness to collaborate. Just telling people to collaborate ignores the reality of our initial feelings of conflict in a negotiation and the need to learn how to approach that conflict. We begin with relationship tension. Hence, you can tell me to collaborate with my counterparty, but that just isn't going to happen.

Collaboration is an end result that only begins once there is sincere care for another's needs, desires, wants, and success—not just yours. This care leads to a desire to understand the other's challenges and opportunities. The process of understanding requires asking, listening, questioning, and clarifying. Through the mutuality of this process engaged in by me and you, the opportunity for collaboration develops. This cycle of caring and engagement leads to trust.

Trust leads to bonding. Once I trust you, I now see an us, a we. Once there is an us and a we, there is a new entity. Bonding leads to belonging. We now belong to this group and have that powerful sense of common purpose and belonging. At this point, collaboration increases and becomes habitual, invisible, and cultural. A collaborative style, a collaborative culture, and a collaborative team are the result of other activities. They come at the end of an evolution of symbiotic and synergistic human behaviors. We need to stop telling people to collaborate and teach them the ingredients and components of collaboration. We need to create structures that support the building blocks and the process of building collaboration. We need to learn and teach how to engage in caring. We need to learn and teach how to turn that care into trust. We need to learn and teach how to turn that trust into a bond from which a new entity (we, us) can emerge. Finally, we then need to reinforce that new entity so we feel we belong to something that should be preserved and perpetuated.

Arguably, that is exactly what happened on Gilligan's Island. Everyone bonded, and the sense of belonging was real. Was that bonding so real that they never really wanted to leave the island? Leaving the island meant destroying that new entity they had created. Maybe sabotaging escape plans was an unconscious way of saying, "We need to stay together." Maybe over those ninety-nine episodes, they succeeded by not getting off of the island. Or maybe, as I said before, the producers and directors were just keeping the characters on the island for self-preservation. Maybe it was a little of both. So often, we don't know what we want. When you put multiple people together, you increase the confusion exponentially.

Likewise, in Istanbul, in our outcome-oriented, positional bargaining situation of buying a scarf, we collaborated. We created a we between us and the scarf vendor. We bonded over stories about our countries, families, and lives. We built trust. We built a situation in which both parties wanted the other happy. This wasn't because our particular result was right or wrong. The result was right for us, and he worked with us toward our happiness. He did the very same thing with the Armani/Rolex crowd. He made them happy. He collaborated with them, but nobody started with trust and collaboration. It came after he asked and listened, and we exchanged life stories.

Who is the Real Team?

Good salespeople don't sell until they learn one thing: Who is the decision-maker? They will make calls, conduct research, and try to understand how their product or service will benefit their prospect, but they will simultaneously try to understand who has the authority, power, and budget to buy what they are selling.

This can be a challenge because power and authority are not necessarily held by just one person. Buying is often done in teams. There may be a procurement representative, a subject matter expert, an end user who needs the product or service, and a few others from different areas who are on loan to the team for objectivity.

As I said previously, I sold aerospace and defense engineering talent and consulting services for twenty years. I always needed to be thinking about the full community with which I was negotiating. Boeing wasn't just the five people in the room I was trying to help with engineering talent on the 787. It was the 787 team, its leadership, and the broader staff all the way up to the CEO. There was Boeing's way driven by Boeing's culture.

You can't understand why the team is not getting off Gilligan's Island until you understand who is really running the show. Aside from the characters, the show's community depends on failure in each episode. The producers, writers, directors, actors, and advertisers all rely on failure for their livelihood. No matter how hard the characters try to get off the island, they won't, and they can't.

You need to understand the community from which your counterparty comes, or you will find yourself scratching your head, wondering why you can't get off the island.

Collaboration, Leadership, and Accountability

No one on the *Gilligan's Island* team had accountability with respect to getting off the island. Skipper was a boat captain, not a survival expert. He may have known how to navigate a ship around islands, but he had no clue about managing on land. When they decided to anoint a leader, they elected Gilligan to run the island. Isn't that perfectly aligned with the objective of not getting off the island? As you consider collaboration, ask yourself, who should lead? Without a leader, there was no accountability for the trials, no learning from episode to episode about what worked and what didn't and what should be done differently. There was no one to tell Gilligan not to touch things (although Skipper was still his direct boss), no one to guide and develop the professor's inventions, and no one to create that powerful single purpose instead of the self-interests that pervaded the characters' behavior.

Collaboration, Roles, and Who is in the Room

Think about the diverse roles among the *Gilligan's Island* characters and how they are actually designed not to work well together. A billionaire and a professor sound like a recipe for greatness. The professor can invent things, and the billionaire can invest in them. But none of that future planning happens (probably because they know they aren't going to get off the island). While they are on the island, the billionaire's money is of no use, and his character is for entertainment only. You would not want that role on your team under these circumstances. Skipper is a fish out of water. He knows seafaring navigation, but this island is "uncharted." So, they don't know where they are to share their location with the outside world. Gilligan is the go-to for ruining a plan. The professor is a scientific genius, but when paired with Gilligan, his inventions often go up in smoke. The next time you are put on a team to collaborate, if you can't control who is on the team, control who is in the room.

As I mentioned earlier, in the summer of 2022, I applied for and was admitted to the Harvard Program on Negotiation Advanced Masterclass. It was a terrific opportunity to face off with fifty-nine classmates from around the world in various negotiation scenarios after we had a chance to learn some of the latest strategies. You will recall I described a multi-party negotiation simulation, where my role was to try to prevent a deal from happening between the parties. I was Gilligan. Without being obvious, it was my job to figure out how the parties might come together and then put obstacles in their way. While everyone was collaborating, I was listening and carefully and clandestinely pushing self-interests of other parties that were inconsistent with good collaboration. It was tricky, challenging, and fun to be Gilligan.

I learned from that exercise that as long as I could keep them in the same room (we were on Zoom), I could create chaos. I lost ground when subgroups agreed to meet privately to work out their differences. The players began requesting to separate into breakout meetings when they had a difference they thought they could resolve. Assume there were eight players, and three needed something from each other or had some inconsistency to work out. If those three could meet separately and focus on just those issues, they would make progress. I wasn't in the room to raise interesting points and challenges to give them pause. Through these breakout sessions, as I previously described, they ultimately reached an overall agreement moments before the end of the negotiating session.

The moral of the story: If you can control who is in the room or "on the island," you can control the outcome. Moreover, if you have trouble understanding the outcome, perhaps you are looking at the five people on the floor or the seven people on the island instead of the broader team or community.

Whether you are using principled negotiation or positional skills, collaboration is important because trust leads to results. Telling two sides to collaborate is inappropriate and ignorant because the parties are adverse. Working on the predicates of trust and collaboration is key. Those predicates begin with listening, asking, caring, and sharing. Further, as you consider collaboration, consider who you are collaborating with. Who is the team, and who is the community? To the extent you can, control who is in the room for successful collaboration.

CHAPTER 11

The Interaction, Movement, and Trajectory of the Seven Tensions

THE SEVEN TENSIONS can be used against each other or with each other. Some naturally complement others. Some are great tools to counter the tension strategies from your opponent. How do you deal, for example, with someone who seems to be reliant on relationship tension as a negotiation tactic? How do you handle someone who brings power to the negotiating table? How should you react to a timing demand? By studying the interactions between the seven tensions, you can learn which tensions to use in response to others.

The seven tensions are dynamic, not static. Over time, one may gain or lose power. Relationships grow or deteriorate. Desired outcomes change over time. The process often changes as the negotiation proceeds. You may change agents, or agents may change their positions. Teams are dynamic, as members can come and go. The movement of the seven tensions may have a natural or predictable trajectory. Some trajectories may, at first, seem random, but through study, you can predict where the tensions are heading.

A criminal defense lawyer recently told me that defendants seek to delay because a prosecutor's case often gets harder as time goes on. Witnesses may no longer be interested in cooperating, evidence gets lost and destroyed, and memories start to fade. So, the trajectory of timing is not favorable for a prosecutor. This might lead to an easier plea bargain for a defendant and certainly affects the negotiations.

Relationship

Relationship tension involves the knowledge and use of the relationship between the counterparties. Negotiations where relationship tension is prevalent can be countered by using other tensions, such as timing, agent, team, or process. A classic negotiation where relationship is paramount involves significant others such as boyfriends, girlfriends, spouses, relatives, and other interpersonal relationships.

One of my favorite failed negotiations involves a hit song by the Beatles called "We Can Work It Out." This song, released in 1965, was written by Paul McCartney with some help from John Lennon. The song was written about Paul's girlfriend, Jane Asher, and a dispute they were having about their life together. Jane Asher was an aspiring actress in London. Upon their engagement, Paul wanted Jane to follow the band like a groupie, and she wanted to continue her career. The song was a message to her that they could "work it out." Let's look at the lyrics:

> *Try to see it my way,*
> *Do I have to keep on talking till I can't go on?*
> *While you see it your way,*
> *Run the risk of knowing that our love may soon be gone*
> *We can work it out,*
> *We can work it out.*
>
> *Think of what you're saying*
> *You can get it wrong and still you think that it's alright*
> *Think of what I'm saying,*
> *We can work it out and get it straight, or say good night*
> *We can work it out,*
> *We can work it out.*
>
> *Life is very short, and there's no time*
> *For fussing and fighting, my friend*
> *I have always thought that it's a crime,*
> *So I will ask you once again*
> *Try to see it my way,*
> *Only time will tell if I am right or I am wrong*
> *While you see it your way*
> *There's a chance that we may fall apart before too long*
> *We can work it out,*
> *We can work it out.*
>
> *Life is very short, and there's no time*
> *For fussing and fighting, my friend*

I have always thought that it's a crime,
So I will ask you once again
Try to see it my way,
Only time will tell if I am right or I am wrong
While you see it your way
There's a chance that we may fall apart before too long
We can work it out,
We can work it out.

Notice the use of other tensions. Timing tension is evident with the lyric, "There is no time for fussing and fighting." Power tension is applied with the lyric, "Run the risk of knowing that our love may soon be gone." Outcome tension is applied with the constant request, or really, the demand, "Try to see it my way." This happy tune with the smiling chorus, "We can work it out," is completely unaligned with the several tensions in the song, including the prospect of ending the relationship, time being of the essence, and only one possible outcome, "my way." The song should more aptly be called "My Way or the Highway." They did not, of course, work it out, as Jane Asher went on the BBC in 1968 with the message, "My engagement to Paul McCartney is officially off."

McCartney's explanation of the lyrics admits that he was being selfish:

> *"It was 1965. Things were not going so smoothly between Jane Asher and me. Everyone has mild arguments where you think, 'God, I wish they could understand where I'm coming from' or 'I wish they could get it.' They obviously don't; they*

think I'm some kind of idiot or tyrant or something. It was just normal boyfriend-girlfriend stuff where she'd want it one way, I'd want it another way and I would try to persuade her, or she would try to persuade me. Most of the time we got on really well, but there would be odd moments where one or other of us would get hurt.

"Time has told me that millions of people got through these little squabbles all the time and will recognize just how common this is, but this particular song was not like that; it was, 'Try to see it my way.' When you're a songwriter, it's a good thing to just go off and get your point of view in a song, and with a Beatles song, if it's going to be heard by millions of people, you can spread a good message: 'We can work it out.' If you wanted to say it in one line, it would be, 'Let's not argue.' If you wanted to say it in two lines: 'Let's not argue/Listen to me.' Obviously that is quite selfish, but then so is the song.

"I started writing the song to try to figure my way out of feeling bad after an argument. It was really fresh in my mind. You can't write this kind of song two weeks later. You have to do it immediately. Writing a song is a good way to get your thoughts out and to allow yourself to say things that you might not say to the other person."

Paul McCartney
The Lyrics: 1956 to the Present

What are some natural methods to combat relationship tension? What tensions can you turn to in response? It isn't uncommon for relationship tension to be met with relationship tension. A significant other may say, "I am leaving," and the response from the counterparty is, "I am leaving, too." As with Paul McCartney and Jane Asher, this is not a successful strategy and tends to throw more fuel on the fire. Successful counter tensions include the introduction of an agent, e.g., a relationship counselor. Another successful counter-tension may be the introduction of a new process by which matters could be resolved. Finally, one person may solicit support from other team (family) members.

Relationships may change over time during the negotiations. In the case of Jane Asher, she simply went on TV, without his knowledge, and ended it, going on to become an even more successful actress, wife, and mother of three children. If relationships are important in a negotiation, then you need to actively monitor their status using the mid-negotiation checklist in Appendix B.

Timing, Outcome, and Power (TOP)

Outcome tension tends to be accompanied by power and timing tension. Someone who is driving an outcome often works leverage and time to get the result they want. This is classic business management. A boss may say, "I want the report, and I want it by Friday." Timing, outcome, and power tensions often travel together.

Let's look at Elon Musk's (a classic TOP negotiator) negotiations with Bret Taylor, the Chairman of the Board of Twitter (now known as X), as evidenced by now-published tweets.

Bret Taylor

Chairman of the Board,

I invested in Twitter as I believe in its potential to be the platform for free speech around the globe, and I believe free speech is a societal imperative for a functioning democracy.

However, since making my investment I now realize the company will neither thrive nor serve this societal imperative in its current form. Twitter needs to be transformed as a private company.

As a result, I am offering to buy 100% of Twitter for $54.20 per share in cash, a 54% premium over the day before I began investing in Twitter and a 38% premium over the day before my investment was publicly announced. My offer is my best and final offer and if it is not accepted, I would need to reconsider my position as a shareholder.

Twitter has extraordinary potential. I will unlock it.

[SEND VIA TEXT]

As I indicated this weekend, I believe that the company should be private to go through the changes that need to be made.

After the past several days of thinking this over, I have decided I want to acquire the company and take it private.

I am going to send you an offer letter tonight, it will be public in the morning.

Are you available to chat?

[VOICE SCRIPT]

1. Best and Final:

a. I am not playing the back-and-forth game.

b. I have moved straight to the end.

c. It's a high price and your shareholders will love it.

d. If the deal doesn't work, given that I don't have confidence in management nor do I believe I can drive the necessary change in the public market, I would need to reconsider my position as a shareholder.

i. This is not a threat, it's simply not a good investment without the changes that need to be made.

ii. And those changes won't happen without taking the company private.

2. My advisors and my team are available after you get the letter to answer any questions

a. There will be more detail in our public filings. After you receive the letter and review the public filings, your team can call my family office with any questions.

Look how Elon Musk uses the outcome, "My offer is my best and final offer," and flexes power, "If it is not accepted, I would need to reconsider my position as a shareholder," and finally, timing tension, "I am going to send you an offer tonight and it will be public in the morning." He even works to throw in a little team tension, "your shareholders will love it."

The Twitter reaction to Musk's TOP approach was initially a TOP reaction. They adopted a poison pill to fight off the acquisition. It is not unusual for a TOP approach to be met with a TOP response. But then, in an about-face, they accepted the offer. Why? During that time period, the stock market dropped significantly, especially technology stocks, including Tesla. Interest rates rose, and the "best and final" began to look like a "worst and get me out of this deal" to Musk.

How do you counter a TOP-driven negotiation or negotiator? All of the remaining tensions are candidates to counter TOP. You can seek to introduce a process. You may hire a powerful agent. You might try to build a relationship. Finally, you may work to build or coalesce a team. As Musk attempted to exit the transaction, Twitter hired lawyers (agent tension), filed a lawsuit (engaged in process), and built support in their shareholder base (team tension). They did not seek to build a relationship with Musk, and the bitterness was exemplified by his termination of every major executive as he took over.

It is interesting to note how timing changed Musk's power trajectory. When he began purchasing Twitter stock in January 2022, Tesla was around 350, near its high of 400. On April 4, when Musk announced his January purchases, Tesla was at a similar level (341.83). However, by the closing date, his Tesla stock was close to 200. His power diminished, and he went from a TOP strategy to a process to exit and to capitulation when he realized he had no valid legal basis to escape the transaction.

One weakness of a TOP approach is that this type of negotiator or negotiation often skips process. In the case of the Twitter acquisition, for example, Musk was so determined to acquire the company that he left out several important steps, all involving due diligence and escape hatches based on what was discovered in due diligence.

An almost opposite set of tensions characterizes more traditional negotiations. I call it the PART approach: process, agent, relationship, and team. The parties agree early to the steps for reaching an agreement and then hire competent agents who lead the process. Relationships are built and respected, and they use other constituents, their firms, and allies to build a formidable team. This was the approach of the Twitter board and executives. While they may have lost the battle, they arguably won the war. At Musk's closing price, Twitter was worth about $44 billion. Various estimates today put the value of X (formerly known as Twitter) at somewhere between $12.5 and 19 billion, or between a third and a half of what Musk paid for it.

The tensions interact with each other, and some tend to traditionally hang together. While there are more than two types of negotiators and negotiations, you can see a great contrast between a TOP and a PART approach with the Twitter acquisition. Musk led with an outcome, leveraging his wealth as power and demanding a timing that drove the transaction. His opposition, the Twitter board, initially responded in a power fashion but quickly adapted to a PART approach. They most likely changed direction because the timing trajectory of Musk's power tension was rapidly changing, as reflected by declining tech markets and rising interest rates. At the end of the day, the PART strategy prevailed.

What is important to keep in mind as you look at the tensions is that they are always moving and not static. Don't assess them as if they will always be what they are. As you approach a negotiation situation, be nimble enough to adapt to changes between tensions and within tensions. When confronted with a tension or set of tensions, don't simply react with the same tension. Consider which other tension may help you counter the tension presented to you.

CHAPTER 12

Tension as a Tool for Discovery in Negotiations

GREAT NEGOTIATORS ARE adept at using tension as a tool in negotiating. Tension can be used to unbalance a counterparty. This may be done by asking for an unreasonably high price (anchoring high) or setting a boundary. Unbalancing a counterparty can uncover backstories and may lead to disruptive change or open up backchannels.

Backstories are matters likely affecting the negotiation but aren't known to the other party. Backchannels are out-of-process exchanges that facilitate progress in a negotiation. An example of an unknown backstory might be that a company has to do a transaction by a certain date or face extra interest payments. An example of a backchannel might be two lower-level employees meeting in a bar for a drink and exchanging information that moves things forward. Whether you are comfortable using tension for these purposes (and you need to learn to be) or not, you need to know how to deal with it when you are faced with it.

When Putin put 100,000-150,000 troops on the Ukrainian border in 2022, that was designed to create tension, and it did across Europe, the US, and the world. What did we do? We watched. Tension has a timing element. When someone plays a tension card, they are trying to force a response. What card do you play back? How do you respond?

Anchoring in Competitive Negotiations

When I was young, there was no internet tool to quickly check a car's price or verify an invoice. There was a sticker and you negotiated from the sticker. Your only basis for value was going to another car lot or reading a newspaper ad to learn about available discounts. But that sticker was an impactful anchor.

For another example, have you been in a store with a clearance section or semi-annual sale? You look at a tag and see you can buy something for half its original price. The discount causes us to put an emphasis on the original price. The anchor has the effect of creating a bias that has some intrinsic value. Suppose you go shopping for a sports coat, and there is one for $250 and another for 50% off $500. Which one do you feel is of greater value? They both cost the same.

When your counterparty drops an anchor, it creates tension in you, especially if it is way more than you want to pay or far less than you want to offer. How do you react to this tension? As I will reiterate many times in this book, there is one simple principle of tension-aware negotiation. When you feel tension, ask yourself, "How can I give this tension to the other side?" Leading a question with the words "why" and "how" are the best ways to move that tension back to the other party.

One of my business partners and I were approached by a potential buyer of a company we owned. My partner was the majority shareholder, but I had a substantial stake. He was seventeen years older than me and retiring soon, so for those reasons, it made sense for him to drive the deal in the background and for me to negotiate it. He said, "We shouldn't take less than $100 million." We didn't have to sell, and while they didn't have to buy, we would represent a cheap entry into the US market for this European company.

I felt tension over the price. I thought it was too high, given where our results were at the time. Examine the tension of who is on the other side of the table here. My partner would be retiring and never had to deal with these people again. Given my age and role in the company, I certainly would stay. I liked these folks, and I liked the deal. Hence, my relationship tension. My partner exhibited no tension, and I don't think he had any. He had no relationship tension. He had concluded that it was likely that we would sell the company, and if we didn't, that was okay with him. So, he also felt no outcome tension. He was in no rush, so he didn't experience timing tension either. He also thought these Europeans needed a nice American company to enter the US market, so he felt he had the leverage and, therefore, had no leverage tension.

I, on the other hand, had all those tensions. I wanted to sell, and I was worried too high an anchor would scare them off. As I imagined potentially working with them, a new tension developed within me. That tension was intermediary or agent tension. Should I try to persuade my partner, for whom I was a partial agent, to reconsider our price? I thought about timing. Our company was a large S Corp and, as a result, had a potential temporary reduction in taxes due to the Trump tax cuts. Selling now, before those expired, led to some timing tension. Also, my partner was in his late 70s with no children seriously involved in the business, and his personal life was, in my opinion, a bit "chaotic." As a result, I felt the full burden of all seven tensions in this deal scenario.

Fortunately, tension can be moved from one person to the other. Have you ever felt someone's tension pass to you? Have you ever passed tension to someone else? Of course you have! Imagine a group of people sitting quietly in a room, and then someone with tension enters the room. Regardless of how intentional they are with a desire to "share" it, the people in the room quickly start to feel it and exhibit it themselves. Knowing this, I identified all my seven tensions and bundled them into a speech to deliver to the potential buyer.

I told them, "My partner says he won't sell for less than $100 million, so don't even think of making an offer at less than that amount. We won't sign it. The company is not for sale. We are looking at a few good years ahead, so we are fine. After those years, he will retire, and we will sell the business. If you want to prepare an LOI for a sale at $100 million, we will sign it."

Notice how I quickly addressed the seven tensions. The relationship, outcome, and timing didn't matter. Leverage on their side was non-existent, and I set forth a process for them. I was off the hook as an agent and had perfect team alignment. I had gone from all seven tensions to none.

Where was the tension now? They needed a relationship with us. They needed to decide if they could reach our ask. Time and leverage were now on our side. Every one of the seven tensions had been moved to them. And I could feel it.

They were quiet for a few days, and we went about our business. After two or three days, they called and said, "Okay, let's draft an LOI for that amount." You could just say my partner anchored high, but there was much more going on when you appreciated the seven tensions. Anchoring created tension in me, and we succeeded in passing the tension to our counterparty. *Tension management point (TMP): Always make the other party make the hard decisions. Do what it takes to pass the tensions you have identified to your counterparty.*

Identifying and Sharing Boundaries

Drawing lines in a negotiation is a common way to create tension. With relationship tension, it might be, "We will never do a partnership if X is involved." For outcome tension, it could be stating a bottom line. "We will never sign for less than $100 million." For process tension, it might be saying, "Give us your best and final offer (BAFO)." For timing tension, it could be similar to process tension. "We must have your

BAFO by Friday at 5 p.m." For leverage tension, it might be putting 100,000 troops on the border. Intermediary tension can be telling an agent that if they don't come back with an offer of X, then don't come back. If you are the agent and you think your client should accept a deal, but they don't want to, you will have tremendous tension as you try to persuade them to "do the right thing." Team tension is very frequent and often happens when team members disagree on a potential outcome. Disagreement over boundaries can invoke all seven tensions, and counterparties who throw down a boundary are knowingly pushing tension on you.

How do you respond when you feel tension from a boundary? After you identify which of the seven tensions you are experiencing, you can test the boundary, and maybe even cross it. Or you can do what my philosophy professor at Carleton College, Perry Mason, suggested. He said, "When you are backed into a corner, you only have two choices, either change the subject or make a distinction." But that is often not available. Sometimes, you have to accept the boundary.

I recall feeling a boundary I couldn't challenge when negotiating with a major aerospace company over a price for services to be rendered. It was awkward because the person in charge of the purchase had worked for my business partner many years ago. He had issues with my partner from his days as an employee but had told me at least three times, "That's water under the bridge."

They were using a procurement tool designed to buy materials for services, which gave me some comfort in knowing we would be treated fairly. You could see everyone's bids, so it was an open auction. We were their biggest provider of these services, and they were our biggest client. It was imperative to keep their business. When the auction closed, we were the lowest bidder. We reviewed our pricing. It was low, but with our volume, we would be fine, though not great.

We moved on to other matters, but later in the day, I received an email from our former employee, now the aerospace procurement lead, saying they wanted to have a call with us. We reassembled in a conference room and took the call. The procurement lead congratulated us and then gave us a new, even lower price. Talk about tension from a boundary! This was pure leverage tension. He was saying, "I have the power."

I said, "Wait, what about the price from the bidding event?"

He replied, "Well, that was just to get to the final negotiation, which is now."

These were not the rules of bidding and engagement we were given. Unflinchingly, I tried to put the tension back on him and said, "Okay, what if we say no to the price?"

He didn't hesitate either. "I strongly recommend you don't do that." He had the leverage and wanted us to feel it. Some kind of revenge toward my partner, I suppose.

I told him we would get back with him. Then, I spoke with my partner, who said we had to accept that price. Lesson to self, when someone says, "It is water under the bridge," the water is not yet under the bridge. Perhaps you are wondering why I didn't report this behavior to the procurement leadership at the company. The chance of provoking backlash from him was too much of a risk. He would be more likely to be promoted since he was saving the company money.

The most common boundary test that happens is "the bottom line." People often wonder, should I have a bottom line? Should I share my bottom line? Or correspondingly, if I am given a bottom line, how should I respond? From my experience as both a principal and an intermediary, the only time you should share a bottom line is if you really mean it. It is so often used as a bluff technique that I don't take the "bottom line" seriously. People frequently step over their bottom line. So, I take Professor Perry Mason's advice and generally change the subject or make a distinction and then return to test the bottom line.

You can use boundaries to create or reinforce tension. For example, I negotiated to buy a luxury condo to renovate and sell. It needed a lot of work. It was the height of COVID, and I made a "no tension" offer of $2,250,000. The seller wanted $3 million but had come down to $2,850,000 during negotiations with me. My tensions were clear—I had none. They had all the tensions. They had to sell to buy another place for retirement. Their waiting list number had come up where they wanted to retire in California. They then responded with a bottom line of splitting the difference of $600,000 to $2,550,000. I told the broker representing them I was waiting to see what happened with COVID and moving to other properties. I wished them well. Two months later, the broker said, "They will do your deal." I felt bad that they could not find another buyer, and I tinkered briefly with the idea of dropping my price but quickly realized that my reputation as a good and fair dealmaker would be forever tarnished. I did the deal and, a year later, realized a nice (but not incredible) profit. *Tension Management Point: Always design and make tension-free proposals. When all the tension is on the other side, let them feel it as they consider their decision.*

Uncovering Backstories – The Ugly Truth of The Iran Hostage Crisis

The most frustrating tension is the tension you can't and don't understand. I am sure you have been in a negotiation and the other party seems crazy . . . they may be acting crazy (Hamlet strategy), so you can't rule that out. But most often, it is because there is something you don't know and may never know.

Jimmy Carter's presidency had several challenges, not the least of which was inflation. However, his biggest crisis as he faced potential reelection to a second term was the Iran Hostage Crisis. In short, Iranian college students stormed the American Embassy on November 4, 1979. Then, President Carter tried both diplomatic negotiations and desperate failed military solutions to no avail. After 444 days, the hostages were ultimately released on January 20, 1981, minutes after Reagan was sworn into office and a day after an agreement was reached, known as the Algiers Accords.

At the time, it was thought that Iran was afraid of Reagan, which led to the release. While not fully accepted by the mainstream, a different story, the "October Surprise Theory," has recently gained traction. Ben Barnes, a former Lieutenant

Governor of the state of Texas and a neighbor of mine for over ten years in Austin, Texas, recently decided to share his story, which was published by *The New York Times* in June 2023. According to Barnes, he and former Texas Governor John Connally visited numerous Middle Eastern countries to put out the word that Iran should keep the hostages until after Reagan took office because they would get a much better deal. There is proof of the trip's occurrence, and Ben Barnes mentioned it to several people at the time. It was never adequately investigated at the time, and now it is too difficult to confirm. But it is clear that Ben Barnes' and John Connally's trip happened, and he heard what he heard and saw what he saw. He even recounts meeting with William Casey, Reagan's campaign manager, upon returning to report on the trip.

Imagine the tension in the Carter Administration's efforts to negotiate a release as they were battling something they just didn't know about. An opponent might be sending messages that are thwarting the negotiations. Reagan's surrogates used multiple tensions, including relationship tension, timing tension, leverage tension, and intermediary tension. Wait a bit. You will get a better deal if you wait, and you will have a better relationship with the President who is coming. There is a strong consensus that the release of the hostages in October could have flipped the election in Carter's favor. Maybe Carter could have or should have uncovered this plot with intelligence sources in the Middle East or in the US.

How do we uncover backstories? How do we learn what we don't know? When you are feeling tension you cannot solve, it is probably because there is something you do not know.

When there is something you don't know, you can use two methods: continuous and improving trial and error (what we commonly do) and/or tension. We often use trial and error, but we need to become comfortable using tension. Here is what that looks like.

I was once a young corporate lawyer at the largest railroad at the time. We were trying to negotiate a renewal of a lease of railcars with a leasing company, which was a financial company headquartered in downtown San Francisco. The railroad financial employees could not get a reasonable renewal, but we really needed the railcars. The tension among the railcar team was high. The backstory here that we did not know was that the leasing company had an analyst who monitored our railcar demand and slack, and they knew we needed the cars, and as a result, they were completely inflexible on terms. We needed to find a way to reverse the tension. After reviewing the existing lease, I discovered it was only days away from expiring, but when I looked at our options for termination, one option was to return the railcars to the lessor. This would not be unusual at the end of a lease. For example, one option with a car lease is to return the car to the dealer. When I asked the railcar experts about the provision, they were incredulous. After I showed it to them, they said, "Nobody does that."

I contacted our operations department and found a way to return the railcars within a block or two of the leasing company. With permission from the railcar negotiators, I contacted the leasing company's law department and told them we were going to find a new source for railcars and that we would be returning the cars per the lease in a few days at the termination of the lease. Note how I applied both timing tension and intermediary tension. The intermediary tension emanates from the simple fact that the lawyers had prepared this document. The lawyers for the finance company said, "You can't do that." When I pointed to the clause (which they wrote), they said, "That was intended to be boilerplate. We can't actually take the cars. We are a finance company."

"Maybe so," I said, "but we are returning the cars to your office, and they should arrive next Friday or Saturday."

Their negotiators reached out to ours and reached a renewal contract a day later. Was this a "win-win" strategy? No, it was not. It was using the tension of a valid contractual but never-used term coupled with timing. It was a positional move that broke a deadlock. Later, the lawyers amended the contract to remove the ability to return the railcars that way. I am sure they (the intermediaries) were blamed for the negotiation being less than expected.

Driving Tension to Open Backchannels

Tension can play another role. It can be used to force new channels of communication, especially when there are teams involved. Suppose the lead negotiators run into a deadlock or the intermediaries run into a deadlock. Then, alternative communications are often enabled.

I was a principal in an M&A transaction with a foreign company. They had hired a large US law firm, and we had hired a large US law firm. The head lawyers on either side were world-class M&A lawyers. No matter what issue arose as we sat around the table, they would clash over objective standards from their experience and practice. One thorny issue arose about how much of a holdback there should be on the purchase price to support the indemnities. When a company is sold, the seller makes many representations and warranties about the company's condition, financials, and potential liabilities. Those are often "guaranteed" by a holdback of a portion of the purchase price. The buyer wanted a holdback of 20%, and our lawyer wanted 5%. They went round and round, citing various ABA Standards and other deals and what was normal. We all sat and listened and watched (while the legal fees grew). Tensions were high. I looked over at the principals on their side, and we collectively shook our heads. It was near the end of the day, so we agreed to get drinks. Over drinks in about ten minutes, we agreed on a 10% holdback for two years without the lawyers. Tension forced the principals to just do it themselves.

In summary, tension can play a wonderful role in progressing a deal or resolving a dispute. You simply need to be aware of it, retrain your instincts to feel it, stay calm, determine the source of the tension, and then work to resolve it or pass it to another party. The very last thing you want to do is to avoid it. That is unnatural.

CHAPTER 13

In Defense of Positional Bargaining

POSITIONAL BARGAINING GOT a bad reputation in *Getting to Yes* and has never recovered. Let's look at the three periods in the history of negotiation: pre-*GTY*, the era of *GTY*, and post-*GTY*.

Pre-GTY

To assess the era before *GTY*, you must go somewhere where negotiation practice hasn't changed for centuries. My favorite place to witness and experience this is the Grand Bazaar in Istanbul, but I have also negotiated in open markets in and around Cancun and Los Cabos, Mexico. I especially like to negotiate for silver and silver pieces in Mexico.

The core negotiation principles of pre-*GTY* negotiation are:

1. Get to know the counterparty so you can develop trust. Relationship is paramount.

2. Enter the negotiation knowing there will be compromises on both sides, which is a good thing.

3. Timing will be whatever it takes to reach an agreement or not.

4. Given 1, 2, and 3, the outcome will not lead to hostility; counterparties will shake hands in the end.

5. Extreme statements may be made, and tension may well occur, but it is not taken seriously. One might say, "My family will starve," in reaction to an offer, but it is intended for effect.

6. Walking away is a perfectly acceptable behavior. Symbolic walking away may lead to a concession.

7. If there are multiple issues, there will be "log rolling." As previously defined, log rolling is a negotiation term that describes a situation with more than one item up for negotiation. In this situation, I may care more about issue A than B or C, and you care more about B and C. You give me A, and I give you B and C.

The Era of *GTY*

This is the era that introduced the outcome/process-based foundations of 1) separating the people from the problem, 2) getting behind interests, not positions, 3) knowing your BATNA, 4) developing multiple options toward mutual gain, and 5) using objective criteria. Fundamentally, there is nothing wrong with the thoughts behind these process tips.

As I previously described, an entire school of thought developed around these principles, called the Program on Negotiation at Harvard Law School. It posits that disentangling (their latest phrase) and separating what people want from their motivations, working those motivations, generating creative ways to jointly problem solve, staying aware of the next best alternative to a negotiated agreement, and introducing objective criteria will win the day. But that is rarely what happens in practice.

First, as we have shown, the *who* matters. The notion of separating the people from the problem leaves behind critical information that may actually help you solve the problem. Knowing the type of person with whom you are dealing, including how they haggle, their biases and culture, and their source of power, is incredibly important. Focusing on creative solutions to underlying motivations is often what positional bargainers do. If you don't want to buy a car that is $50,000 and you keep pushing for $40,000, a positional bargainer will offer you a different car. Keeping your alternative in mind if you don't reach a deal is not original. It is basic to all deal-making and conflict resolution. Introducing objective criteria is not a solution. In fact, in real-life negotiations, nobody just folds once you introduce objective criteria that support your position. Quite the opposite, they will go get their own "objective criteria."

After GTY

The worst thing *GTY* did was dehumanize negotiating humans. It worked to strip our instincts, tensions, and emotions from what is inherently emotional. These emotions can be found in billion-dollar deals, inter-country conflicts, intercultural conflicts, and more. Why should we set these emotions aside? Why should we ignore these tensions? What if we trained people to recognize and manage these tensions instead?

Conclusion

I am advocating for a unification of two very different schools of thought. The concept of joint, dispassionate problem solving, as reflected in the *GTY* era, is aspirational but only applies in certain formats—it doesn't help us with splitting $100, for example. It also doesn't work when you face a counterparty that is determined to engage in positional bargaining with you. Many aspects of complex negotiations have positional components. What *Seven Tensions* really brings to the table is a framework for dealing with the tensions we feel when we negotiate. That framework unifies *GTY* with the other elements of negotiating.

In philosophy, there were rationalists who thought that reason was the sole basis for truth and reality. Along came empiricists who believed that until you experienced something, you could not know what it was or that it was real. Along came Immanuel Kant, who said both were true but had limits. This is exactly the issue with principled versus positional bargaining. You need to be good at both.

CHAPTER 14

Dynamic Tension: How to use Tension as a Sword and Shield

TO MASTER THE art of the seven tensions, you need to be able to both create and manage tension. The seven tensions help you gain power in a negotiation, and if used correctly, you can wield them like a sword. Let's consider the simple example of buying a car.

Relationship Tension: The salesperson is trained and does this for a living. They know way more than you know and owe you nothing. They know more about the car. They know more about the market for the car. They know more about the typical customer of the car. They know how to sell you. If anything, they are expected to be a little sneaky by reputation.

Outcome Tension: The salesperson will deal with lots of customers on any given day. While they would like to sell you a car, if it is a popular car, they will see dozens like you. Unless there is a sales contest or their job is on the line, they are fine. You, however, wanted to get this done today and allocated time for it. They will say they care about your happiness, but you have more at stake because you will drive that car every day.

Timing Tension: Buying a car the traditional way takes a long time. Dealerships are masterful at drawing out the process. They have a system. You have a Saturday afternoon. Timing generally favors them.

Power Tension: We have already discussed the basis for power tension, but the remaining tensions can be played to exacerbate and increase the power tension in negotiations.

Process Tension: The dealership controls the negotiation process. You enter the dealership and wander around a bit, looking at cars. A salesperson watches you and decides when to engage. They ask you questions, and you respond. If you are a good negotiator, you ask them good questions. It is not impossible to take control of the process, but it is unusual because you only do this once every three or four years. Once you begin to negotiate, it is all about them. Your salesperson might tell you they have to talk to finance and then to the manager, and the back and forth will wear you down until your guard is lowered. Then, it's game over.

Agent Tension: The salesperson is an agent and plays it well. They get to leave you and talk to the principal while you sit in their office and wonder what you are doing. None of this is an accident. It is designed as a method of control.

Team Tension: Who is your team? In this scenario, you generally don't have one. They have a professional dealership with a team working sales, a team working finance, and a team working "the stage."

Considering all seven tensions, you can see why dealerships have all the power. The deck is stacked against you before you get out of bed that Saturday.

Now, let's consider how we can flip the script, use the sword, and make the dealer make the hard decision instead of you.

How to Leverage Tensions to Gain Power: Flipping the Script

Relationship Tension: Do your research on the dealership, the car, the market for the Q5, and the salesperson if you can. How is the dealership financially? Is there a surplus of Q5s or a shortage? What is the real MSRP? Are there enhancements to this car in the works so a new model will come out soon? How long has this sales manager been selling cars? You can change the relationship by putting yourself on a near-equal basis with regard to knowledge because there is so much information available.

Outcome Tension: You care about the outcome more than they do. However, you can demand your happiness and not care about the dealership or salesperson's happiness. I always ask for the most experienced salesperson they have. I do that because they have less outcome tension. The fewer cars you sell, the more pressure on each one. Volume salespeople are volume salespeople because they produce happy, returning customers. Never work with a rookie.

Timing Tension: Change your position on timing. Psychologically prepare yourself for a no-deal scenario. Make timing work for you. See my example in Chapter VI. You can flip the script on timing by being honest with yourself, knowing you have time, and not treating it like an emergency. You can tell the salesperson you will buy a car in the next six months, but probably not today. Prepare them and prepare yourself to take their timing power away.

Power Tension: Your power tension can be reduced by having lots of choices. Visit every dealer. Do great searches online. Talk to lots of people. And most importantly, flip the script on all six of the other tensions.

Process Tension: You can decide the process. You do not have to let them drive the process. If they say, "Let's take a test drive," you might say not yet or no. If they say, "Let me go talk to my manager," you say, "Let's keep talking, just the two of us. I don't want to play that game." If they start throwing finance deals at you, you say, "Let's agree on a price for the car before we talk about how I will pay for it." You resist their game and insist on yours.

Agency Tension: Don't shop alone and always have a "principal." One of my favorite negotiation jokes goes like this:

A man goes to buy a car. He negotiates the price just like our above example. The dealer starts at $60,000. The customer reacts with $52,000. The salesperson says, "I know they won't go that low, but let me see what they will do."

He returns five minutes later and says, "Good news, they will go to $58,000." The man matches their concession and goes to $54,000. The salesperson says, "Give me a minute." Ten minutes later, he returns with a $57,000 counter. This time, they have prepared a contract with this price on it. "They are serious," he says. "Look, it is in writing." The salesperson puts it in front of the man. The man studies the contract. The man is near his reservation point, which he now offers at $54,435. The salesperson says, "I will be right back." Fifteen minutes later, he reappears and says they will split the difference and has a contract in hand for $55,717.50. Plus, they will throw in a wheels and tire warranty, which is nearly $1,000 in value. He smiles. The man says, "Okay, thank you very much. Now, I need to go check with my wife." The man has set up his wife as a principal, and he is the agent.

Team Tension: There is no rule that you have to go shopping for a car alone. You should always take someone with you. You need your own team that counters theirs. One of my former business partners and I used to enjoy buying our company cars together. We would play off each other and keep the salesperson guessing who the decision maker was, what we would do, what we were thinking, and pretty much everything you would try to learn about your counterparty(ies) that I recommend. Once, we were at a Porsche dealership in Dallas, Texas. We wanted to buy two new Porsche 911S coupes. After driving a salesperson crazy and reaching his, "We can't do anymore point," we said, "Okay, have a nice day, and we left." We started to chat next to our cars in the parking lot. We chatted about the Cowboys and how frustrating they were, the weather, and future travel, and we continued talking until the sales manager, who we had not met, came hustling out of the dealership (as we knew he would).

He said, "Hey guys, where y'all going? I am the sales manager. What is the problem?"

We told him, "No problem. We just couldn't reach a deal with your rep."

He said, "Why don't you come back in. I am sure we can work it out."

We said, "No, we are fine. If you want to match our offer, we will still do it."

He countered with, "Well, let's come inside and see if we can do that."

Again, we reiterated, "No, we are fine."

At this point, he informed us that he would be right back. He came back out with two sales contracts for the price we wanted, and we bought the cars.

You can change the dynamics of a deal by understanding the seven tensions and using them to flip the script. The dealership made a tough decision that day. We were fine. The sales manager was smart, though. We bought many cars on our reasonable and researched terms from that manager. He never made us come to the dealership. He brought the paperwork to us. Who controlled the relationship, outcome, process, timing, power, agency, and teamwork?

We did! And you can, too!

Control over a negotiation is not about having a better BATNA, applying psychological pressure, or using authority. It is about understanding and applying the seven tensions framework. It is about breaking the tensions down and identifying which you are driving and which are being driven against you.

CHAPTER 15

Negotiator Tension Archetypes

NEGOTIATORS OFTEN HAVE a dominant tension they use when leading negotiations. Being able to identify dominant tensions in others can help you negotiate more successfully. Let's consider the seven tensions and the style of negotiator who leads with each tension.

Relationship Tension Archetype—Former President Donald J. Trump

A relationship negotiator believes that anything can be solved by simply using the power of relationships. These negotiators believe their personality, ability, charisma, and omnipotence can solve any negotiation problem. The archetype of this style is former president Donald J. Trump. Based on accounts from those closest to him during his administration, President Trump was not concerned with the substance (he barely listened to briefings), nor process or timing. His sole variable for success was getting into a room and developing a relationship with other world leaders or whomever he wanted to negotiate, including Putin, Xi, or even Kim Jong Un. Once he developed a relationship, they would agree, get in line, see it his way, etc.

Relationship negotiation correlates with classical narcissism. Ovid's poem *Metamorphoses* describes the hunter who fell in love with his own reflection. The relationship with oneself is so powerful that the belief in the relationship becomes dominant.

Former President Trump is just one obvious example of the relationship archetype. It is a type that is common in political circles. "Just put me in the game, Coach," they think. President Bill Clinton was also a high relationship tension archetype. Where you find charisma, you tend to find this archetype. With this strong belief in themselves, the relationship negotiator archetype often goes hand in hand with the use of power tension. But power is used after developing a relationship. You can contrast this type of negotiator with other types when you compare more politicians.

Outcome Tension Archetype

Contrast that strongly with former President Jimmy Carter. Carter negotiated by doing his homework and reading everything at his disposal. Carter was an outcome tension archetype. He thought and studied deeply about what the result should be and worked counterparties through his research and analysis to help them arrive at his conclusion. His classic negotiation between Israel and Palestine in the Camp David Accords in 1978 was not based on his charisma but on his work and homework. He drew up a U.S. peace proposal (the outcome). Then, when Begin and Sadat didn't want to be in the same room, Carter took them to Gettysburg (an emblem of a horrible outcome) to show what would happen if negotiations failed. He met with their teams without the two leaders and took copious notes.

Consider the stark contrast between Trump and Carter as an example of the contrast between the outcome archetype and the relationship tension negotiator archetype. Outcome archetypes often focus on the process. Relationship negotiators don't need a process; they just need themselves. Outcome negotiators choose an outcome and adjust their processes to achieve results. Relationship archetypes are among the least prepared. Why should they be? Their presence is enough. On the other hand, outcome and process archetypes are the most prepared.

Agent Tension Archetypes

Career lawyers are agent archetypes. They can take any position and shape it into a compelling position. They spend their lives taking up the mantle of their clients. They are indifferent to the substance of the position and design an outcome and processes around achieving the client's objectives.

Timing Tension Archetype

I saw the timing archetype up close and personal with one of my key business partners. He was an engineer by training. He wasn't charismatic, yet a quiet introvert. He actually believed he wasn't well-liked, which wasn't true, so he didn't rely on his personality. However, his timing was amazing. He was patient and waited to get his way or negotiate. Like a lobster under a rock, he waited for what he wanted to come along and then pounced on it. If anyone tried to push him at any other time, he would just shut down and do nothing.

Team Tension Archetype

Team archetypes are corporate, government, and labor negotiators. They only work in teams and would never think of negotiating alone. They negotiate like bureaucrats. I have noticed that different cultures rely on team negotiations more heavily than others. For example, my experiences while negotiating with Japanese companies definitely reflected the team archetype. Nobody ever negotiated with me singularly. There would be meetings with team members, never one-on-one, but the meetings, as it was explained to me by the company leadership, were just to gather information. They did not make a decision until they had a larger group consensus. As a result, they moved very slowly. But when they moved, they moved with confidence and strength.

As a cleared company, we dealt with the US Defense Department frequently. Every person we engaged with was a team archetype. There was never just one person in a room. There was also never an opening to make a decision while in the negotiating room because the team was bigger than the people in the room.

The Union Pacific Railroad I joined in 1985 was team-driven. I believe they were team-driven because many of the management structures and the culture reflected military order. During WWI, the railroads were nationalized. Participants from the railroad side even had instructions on when to enter the room and in what order for a meeting. We entered meetings in reverse order of seniority and importance and left the room in order of seniority and importance. Decisions were not made in the meeting; only discussions were had. Then, we met as a team and made a joint decision, which was relayed back to our counterparty.

Power Tension Archetype

Power archetypes include leaders like Putin, Xi, and Kim Jung Un. Dictators are classic power archetypes. When threatened, power archetypes respond with force. For example, power on power could involve North Korea launching a missile at another power negotiator, with their response being a counter-strike or threat. Netanyahu is this type of negotiator. Negotiation through force.

In contrast, relationship archetypes respond by showing up and calling a meeting. No matter what they face, even force, they work the relationship. While Trump may look like a power archetype at first glance, he is a relationship archetype. When North Korea launched missiles, Trump didn't show counter strength. He arranged a meeting because he believed he could get into a room and develop a relationship, and everything would be fine. Note that among the classified documents he kept were his letters from Kim Jung Un. He was all about the relationship.

Conclusion

It is important to try to ascertain the archetype of the negotiator with whom you will or are negotiating. It will help you immensely in your negotiations. If you try approaching Donald Trump (relationship negotiator) as if he were Jimmy Carter (outcome and process negotiator), you will put him to sleep. Likewise, if you try to reason with a power negotiator, you will be disappointed and confused when he or she attacks you.

CHAPTER 16

Classic Negotiating Questions and the Seven Tensions

THE SEVEN TENSIONS framework can help you answer some fundamental questions that arise when negotiating deals and disputes. Without a framework, negotiators tend to go with their instincts or make it up as they go along. The purpose of this chapter is to apply the seven tensions framework to these common questions:

- Who should go first?
- How should I handle impasse?
- Should I ever split the difference?
- Is bluffing a good thing to do?
- When should I walk away?

We will address each of these in turn.

Who Should Go First?

There is a negotiation adage that says, "He who goes first loses." The point of the adage is that whoever speaks first shows their cards and intentions and exposes themselves to an easy counter. If you are buying and your number is higher than it needs to be, your counterparty might just say yes. The same is true if you are selling and your number is lower than it needs to be. It is also possible that your number is completely outside the other party's, and now there will be no deal. The theory is that you simply expose yourself, and your counterparty can take advantage of that.

However, there are also schools of thought that say you should always go first. This gives you an opportunity to take control of the negotiation. You can "anchor high" (set a high price) if you are selling or alternatively "anchor low" if you are buying. The same applies to a settlement.

Retailers do not hesitate to "go first." Have you ever seen a car at a dealership without a price or sticker on it? Probably not. They use that sticker to take control and anchor high. Since they have set the price, they also set the sale or discount amount. They control the negotiation in part by controlling the factors that lead to the outcome.

So, who is right? The answer is both and neither; there are occasions where you should go first and occasions where you should not. (Note that regardless of whether you should go first, you should always be prepared to go first.) But how can you determine when to do what? The seven tensions can guide us.

Parties in a power position who control the timing, process, and outcome tensions often start negotiations. Let's consider a couple parties in this type of position. First, a bank. If you want a loan from a bank, you need to follow their process. They set the timing and decide whether to give you a loan or not. They tell you the interest rate, how much they will loan you, and what the term of that loan will be. You may compete some banks against each other to try to change those terms, but those terms tend to be fairly similar between banks. They have the money and the power.

A second example of a power position is a car dealer. They control the same three tensions and have substantial leverage. That is why stickers, financing deals, and terms are posted everywhere and even advertised on TV.

In both scenarios, there are a couple observations worthy of note. First, there is no relationship between the parties. Second, they are controlling the process as well. If you want the loan or the car, you have to do what they tell you when they tell you. Putting the price forward is consistent with them controlling everything else. So, when you are in the power position, controlling the power, timing, process, and outcome, you should be comfortable maintaining your control by putting forth a price. You are working to control all the tensions; there is no need for you to be weak on any given element.

But what if there is a relationship between the parties? Let's take a couple of common relationships between parties: superior and subordinate in a work environment and a parent and child. Who makes the first offer here? In a relationship, it tends to be the one who wants something. If an employee wants a raise, the employee will ask for a raise. If the child wants to borrow a car or go somewhere, they will ask. In the case of the subordinate asking for something, they will lean on the relationship to advocate on their behalf. "I really like working here, but . . ."

Timing can play a role in who goes first, too. If you look at the source of your power and become worried that it might deteriorate, then you might go first because time is of the essence. Elon Musk didn't hesitate to go first in the Twitter acquisition because he was in a power position (his wealth, the source of his power, was at a peak). He drove the outcome and dictated the process. As the source of his power deteriorated with the declining markets and his wealth, he regretted that decision tremendously. So, make sure you understand the likely power trajectory (for both or all parties) before you initiate an offer.

While you should always be prepared to go first, whether you go first or not depends on your preparation around the seven tensions. Make sure you consider the relationship, timing, power, process, and outcome so you develop a good plan. Even the team and agent tensions can come into play. For example, you can use an agent to balloon an initial offer. You can also blame your team in front of your counterparty if your initial offer is rebuffed.

How Should I Handle Impasse?

It is not unusual for a deal to bog down at some point, with counterparties threatening to quit or go dark. Sometimes, they just go silent. How can you bring them back to the deal? What strategies can you use among the tensions to reengage?

Step one is to identify which of the seven tensions led to the impasse. Did someone hurt someone's feelings (relationship)? Did the process break down? Did an agent cause the impasse? Did a member of their team or your team cause the issue? Did it take too long, or was it going too quickly (timing)? Did someone decide they were not going to get the outcome they wanted? Did someone over-exercise their power?

Once you identify the cause of the impasse, then you can address that cause by solving the tension. If there is a relationship, you will obviously work that. You will appeal to the trust you have built during the relationship. You might apologize if appropriate. If the timing was off, you need to recalibrate and see if you can reset time expectations or agree to move more quickly or slowly. If the process wasn't working, you can establish a new process. If a team member was a problem, you can remove them or ask that they be removed.

Solving an impasse is all about identifying the root cause of the tension and then solving that specific tension. If the tension is on your side, is there a way to flip the script and return the tension to them to solve the impasse? If they say they have to have an answer by Wednesday, you can feel free to say you can't make a decision until Saturday. Instead of creating stress by figuring out how to respond by Wednesday, they now have to make the hard decision to respect an extension.

Should I Ever Split the Difference?

Great negotiators split the difference all the time. It is rare at the beginning, but at some point in the process, it will be an efficient way to resolve an outstanding issue. The seven tensions can help you decide when and how to split the difference in a negotiation.

If there is a relationship that will be ongoing, splitting the difference establishes a grounding of fairness. Nobody ever got fired for bringing back half the candy bar. No relationship ever broke down because it was only fifty-fifty. But I do agree that if done too early, splitting the difference can be lazy and lead to a bad result. While splitting the difference can be fair and effective, the first to do it will often get less than their target. When you do it matters. I disagree with Chris Voss in *Never Split the Difference,* who says, "Splitting the difference is wearing one black and one brown shoe, so don't compromise. Meeting halfway often leads to bad deals for both sides." However, splitting the difference when a relationship is at stake is nearly always appropriate.

If there is no relationship between the parties, the more powerful party will split the difference as long as it is above their reservation point. Car dealers are always splitting differences, but only because the split is within the deal they want. Offer a deal outside of their zone of an acceptable price, and they will not split the difference. By splitting the difference while in their acceptable deal zone, they are making themselves look and sound fair but are just having fun in their deal zone.

Is Bluffing a Good Thing to Do?

Bluffing in a negotiation context means "trying to deceive someone as to one's intentions." (Oxford Languages). Many negotiations involve bluffs. Do they work? If so, under what circumstances? What if there is a relationship? What if I bluff about the time or outcome? What if I bluff about process? The type of tension involved is instructive as to whether and how to bluff and what to do if your bluff is called.

If there is a relationship, then a bluff can be very dangerous. The definition of bluff includes the word "deceit." How does deceit generally affect a relationship? If you bluff in a scenario with an important relationship, you may never recover from the loss of trust. This should be taken into account as you consider your strategy.

Bluffing is often used to deal with outcome tension. If the car dealer won't come down to your price, you might say, "If you can't do it for $40k, I will buy somewhere else." If you mean that, fine. But if you don't, and you really want the car, it is going to be awkward whether they say $42k and you say, "Okay, I am out of here," or if you say, "Done." If you leave, then it wasn't a bluff, but you didn't get the car you wanted. If you stay, your bluff was called.

In commercial transactions, outcome tension bluffs are used extensively in negotiations when parties claim BAFO, best and final. Parties will put forth a number as if it is their BAFO, but it is often not. I have seen this on both sides of a commercial transaction. Usually, if you get really close to the BAFO, then that is enough, just like in the car example above.

Agent tension is a common way to play a bluff. Agents are perfect for carrying out a bluff because you can always distance yourself from your agent. Agents, especially lawyers, are free to bluff under the Model Rules of Professional Conduct, but they can't lie. So, if you are going to use your agent, you need to be aware of this restriction. Generally speaking, if there is a document somewhere that says A, your agent can't say "not A." If you want your lawyer to say they think you won't take less than $15 million for the property you are selling, they can do that. But if they ask if you have an appraisal and you want your lawyer to say it is for $15 million, but it is for $10 million, the lawyer cannot ethically do this. Of course, you really can't lie either; otherwise, you may find yourself accused of fraud and face some serious penalties.

Bluffing is a great thing to outsource to an agent, but it is dangerous in the presence of a relationship. Be wary of the tactic, and if you plan to use it, make sure it is in your negotiation plan and preparation. Employing it on the spot and without a plan is a high-risk strategy that can break trust and, if caught, can be embarrassing and kill a deal.

When Should I Walk Away?

Great negotiators walk—frequently. Walking is the best way to know whether you got a good deal or not. Even in a relationship, you can walk. If you can't get the salary you need from your employer, then you take another job. If the car dealer won't meet your price, you go to another dealership. Walking preserves the integrity of your deal. Of course, to walk, you need choices; this is where *GTY* provides great value with its concept of BATNA. You can walk if you have identified and qualified your best alternative to a negotiated agreement.

Walking away from a deal where there is a relationship between the parties doesn't kill the relationship if it is done right and with integrity. In fact, it could help the relationship. If there is a candy bar between us and it is to be shared, but I demand 70% of it, you may walk away and say, "Fine, then you have it." If there is care and trust in the relationship, the greedier party may well reconsider before taking the entire bar. You have to assess the quality of the relationship and how it will be impacted before you leave the table.

When you will walk away should be built into your preparation. Is there a walkaway outcome? Is there a walkaway time? For example, "If I can't get what I want or need by Friday, then I will break off the negotiation." You need to consider each of the seven tensions to make sure you have thought through the appropriate use of the tactic.

Conclusion

When considering how to handle some of the recurring and common issues in a negotiation, run the circumstances through the seven tensions and see what they tell you about the use of each tactic described in this chapter. While not all seven tensions will necessarily determine whether you should or should not use a tactic, some will help you avoid making a tactical error in your negotiation.

CHAPTER 17

The Seven Tensions and
The Twitter Acquisition

ELON MUSK'S ACQUISITION of Twitter will be studied for many years. It is a perfect case study of what not to do. It is surely one of the most poorly negotiated transactions in modern history. Fascinating in its failure, a seven-tensions analysis highlights the missteps. Analyzing the improper use of the seven tensions in the transaction confirms the value and integrity of the seven tensions.

The acquisition has all of the drama of a Shakespearean tragedy. The major characters are as follows:

- Elon Musk – Purchaser, entrepreneur, and one of the world's richest people
- Jack Dorsey – Founder and ex-CEO of Twitter
- Parag Agrawal – CEO of Twitter, engineering background
- Bret Taylor – Chairman of the Board of Twitter, seasoned tech entrepreneur

- Yoel Roth – Head of Site Integrity of Twitter

Timeline of the 2022 Acquisition:
- Late January – Musk starts to invest in Twitter.
- March 14 – Musk's stake in Twitter reaches 9.5%, making him the largest shareholder (unannounced and non-public).
- March 25 – Musk publishes Twitter Poll – do we need a new platform?
- March 26 – Jack Dorsey and Elon Musk begin texting.
- March 31 – Dinner between Parag, Bret, and Elon.
- April 4 – Musk files with the SEC, publicly disclosing his acquisition of a 9.5% stake in Twitter.
- April 5 – Parag announces Musk will join the Twitter Board of Directors.
- April 10 – Musk says he will not join the Twitter Board of Directors.
- April 14 – Musk offers to buy Twitter at $54.20 per share, a 38% premium over the price on April 3, the day before his investment was made public.
- April 15 – Twitter adopts a poison pill (a standard takeover defense that makes an acquisition much more expensive) to prevent the Musk acquisition.
- April 21 – Musk publicly announces that he has $46.5 billion in financing for the purchase (SEC filing).
- April 25 – Twitter accepts Musk's offer.
- April 29 – Musk sells $8.5 billion of Tesla stock.
- May 4 – Musk secures $7 billion from various investors.

- May 13 – Musk places the deal on hold due to the prevalence of bot and spam accounts.
- May 26 – Twitter shareholders sue Musk, as Twitter's stock fell more than 12%.
- June 6 – Musk demands more information regarding "bots."
- July 8 – In an SEC filing, Musk moves to terminate the acquisition, and Twitter declares him in breach of the acquisition agreement.
- July 12 – Twitter sues Musk in Chancery Court in Delaware.
- July 19 – Trial date set for October 2022.
- Oct 4 – Musk agrees to continue the original deal.
- Oct 28 – Musk closes the transaction the day before the trial's start date and immediately fires top executives.
- Nov 4 – Twitter begins to lay off half its workforce.

Seven Tension Analysis

Applying the seven tension analysis to the Twitter debacle provides a new framework for understanding what went wrong and why. In the absence of such a framework, people just tend to blame external circumstances, the powerful economic shift, or Musk's idiosyncratic personality and hubris. However, this framework provides more specific detail and constructive feedback. In addition to this, applying the framework in such an extreme and recent failed negotiation shows the integrity of the framework.

Relationship Tension

A good relationship can be key to a positional or principled negotiation. In Twitter's case, both sides failed to recognize the power that could come from understanding each other's motivations, needs, and interests. This not only led to a bad deal for Musk and his investors but also to horrible post-deal execution. While Twitter's management did get their shareholders a great price, from a social perspective, Twitter, now X, is a pale reflection of its former self.

Musk did not have a relationship with Twitter's senior management, but he did have a relationship with the founder, Jack Dorsey, who was ousted, allegedly at the hands of Elliot Management, a major shareholder. Due to the litigation, it came to light that Dorsey and Musk were texting. It is clear that Dorsey was encouraging Musk to acquire Twitter. According to sources, Parag knew Dorsey and Musk had a relationship and were texting, but Parag did nothing about it, nor did he attempt to reengage with Dorsey. As a result, no relationship developed, which could have helped in a proper transition of Twitter post-acquisition.

For his part, Musk did not work to engage in any relationship with management, therefore missing the opportunity for a friendly deal that may have saved him lots of money and prevented the fiasco that followed. Worse yet, as you can see from the timeline, when Musk had dinner with Parag and Taylor on March 31, he had already purchased 9.5% of the company but didn't tell them. They found out about it with the public on April 14 and were blindsided.

Process Tension

Partly due to the lack of any relationship between the parties, no organized process was agreed upon for the acquisition, its consummation, or post-acquisition transition. As a result, the deal was on—as a surprise to Twitter's executives—and then it was off. The tumultuousness following the post-SEC disclosure of the stake was incredible. Musk was suddenly going to be on the board. Then, he was not. Then he made a surprise offer, followed by an attempt to find an escape hatch. A court proceeding. A closing. The failure to establish an agreed-upon process or plan was instrumental in the deal's failure and post-acquisition disaster.

Outcome Tension

It is important that the parties involved in a transaction or negotiation know what they want. If they don't know their goal, they must engage with their team and counterparty to figure it out. That work and discussion did not happen on either side in this transaction.

Neither party knew what it wanted. Musk made the original $3 billion investment, apparently without a plan, while markets were rising in early 2022. He originally just wanted to influence the company as its largest shareholder, and then, days later, he decided to pay $44 billion for all of it. Some of his words were altruistic, claiming he wanted to create a true public marketplace of ideas, but in the end, it very much became Musk's marketplace of ideas. According to reports, when Biden got more reactions to a Superbowl tweet in

February 2023 than Musk did, Musk ordered the engineers to emphasize Musk's tweets in the algorithms that drive what users see.

In their own indecisiveness, instead of initially accepting Musk's offer, Twitter decided to oppose it with a poison pill, a standard defense to a hostile takeover attempt that makes a transaction much more expensive. They did not engage in meaningful discussions about a post-Musk world. Within ten days, they did an about-face and accepted Musk's offer.

Power and Timing Tension

In this negotiation, as in many negotiations, power tension changed rapidly over time, making the two tensions strongly interlinked. Who had the power in this transaction? Early on, there is no question that Musk had the power. He quietly and almost deceitfully became the largest shareholder, using his incredible wealth to buy 9.5%, or $3 billion, of Twitter. However, the markets began to deteriorate, and interest rates began to rise that spring. When Twitter accepted the deal, Tesla stock dropped 12%. When Musk then sold $8.5 billion of Tesla stock, it dropped even further. The source of Musk's power was his wealth, but his wealth was plummeting as Tesla stock fell. As his power fell, his interest in the deal fell because the substantial revaluation of assets dramatically affected both his buying power and the value of what he was buying. When he closed the transaction, his power rose (because now he was firmly in control), and he fired all the executives and then half the staff. The rollercoaster continued, and his power fell as he got rid of many of the very people he needed and others resigned. His power decreased so much that when he got on the stage with Dave Chappelle in San Francisco in January 2023, he was roundly booed.

Initially, Twitter was powerless, although it did fight back with a poison pill. However, once management came to their senses, they accepted the offer in the best interests of the company's shareholders and, ultimately, got a price that was undeniably attractive. They lost power as Musk swooped in with his kitchen sink, but at that point, the company and Musk were one. Many valuable folks resigned, essentially letting go of the rubber band that each side had been tugging. Musk attempted revenge on them with the Twitter Files release, but it's unclear whether anyone was really surprised by Twitter's liberal slant.

Team Tension

Musk brought his team together, but that didn't make him a team player. The engineers from his other companies and some of his relatives were brought into the loop, but by most accounts, their job was to help Musk do what he wanted, not *change* what he wanted.

The Twitter team was more coherent, but sources indicate they had gotten fairly self-satisfied. There wasn't coherence on either side. Engaging their shareholders to enforce the terms of the deal was definitely a team move that worked. Bringing a team together against an otherwise powerful adversary is a smart move and a hallmark of one of the seven tensions.

Agent Tension

Apparently, Musk doesn't like agents. He does everything himself. A lawyer would not let you send texts about the purchase like he did. These texts provide no outs for due diligence (which came back to haunt him). They provided none of the protections a lawyer would insist upon. There was nothing more than, "I am going to buy your company for this amount, and I am announcing it in the morning."

The Twitter lawyers were much more adaptive. Wachtel Lipton initially advised to fight the acquisition with a poison pill defense. A poison pill allows existing shareholders to buy shares at a discount, effectively diluting the value of the shares purchased by the acquirer. However, Wachtel quickly changed course and engaged in litigation to force Musk to close the deal. By all accounts, they were successful, and Musk caved on the eve of the trial. Clearly, hiring the right agents and using those agents skillfully was a smart way to handle the dynamic and tumultuous transaction.

Both sides could have done much better in negotiations had they consciously used the seven-tension framework. Musk relied on three of the tensions: power, outcome, and timing. He ignored process, relationship, agent, and team. These tensions could have saved him. Likewise, Twitter ignored relationship tension. They blew the opportunity in the March 31 meeting, which could have led to a more intelligent outcome for everyone. In many other respects, they played the tensions well, especially agent, team, and process. Economic circumstances also provided them with an advantage as stock markets declined and interest rates rose, causing them to pivot from a power fight to an agent and team-driven legal process.

CHAPTER 18

Positional Bargaining Math

IN NEGOTIATIONS, THERE are lots of opportunities to use basic math. Sadly, many lawyers do not like math, and that is part of the reason they became lawyers. Often, they are highly articulate but not a fan of playing with numbers. You will not find an analysis of negotiation math in books like *Never Split the Difference* (Voss in *Never Split the Difference* does admit on page 205 that, "Negotiation still comes down to determining who gets which slice of the pie, and from time to time you're going to be forced into some real bare-knuckle bargaining with a hard-ass haggler.") However, it is an essential aspect of negotiating. In my experience, sadly, many negotiators don't think through the likely moves and countermoves that could occur in basic price or value negotiations.

Let's begin with how positional bargaining math is frequently done wrong. Let's use a car transaction. Suppose the sticker on a car is $50,000, and your research says its range of value is $44K-$48K. Many people will offer the low end of the range (mistake number one). After the dealer tells you his or her team will never go that low, he will likely counter at the high end of the range. In fact, he may show you an invoice with that amount. Now, you are at $44K, and the dealer is at $48K. What is your next move? You will be tempted to split the difference because it puts you in the middle of what your research says the value is (mistake number two). When you offer $46K to split the difference, you have both sanctioned splitting the difference and set a new mid-point at $47K, which the dealer will likely offer to split the difference again and bring you a contract for that amount, ready to shake your hand. Of the $4K range of value, the dealer gave up $1K, and you gave up $3K.

Let's examine the two errors. First, if you want to end up on the low end of the range, you need to start outside of the range. Please note that the dealer did precisely this. The dealer's sticker is $2K above the range, meaning you should begin at least at an equivalent place. Your initial offer should not be more than $42K. If he or she laughs, you can share your research with them and show them you are no more out of the range than they are. When you offer $42K, they will likely only move down $1K or $2K to show you that you are nowhere near the final deal price. Suppose they now come to the top of the range, $48K. Now, you are $6K apart.

Now, let's avoid mistake number two. If you offer to split the difference, you will now be at $45K, and they will be at $48K. If they split the difference with you again, the deal would be at $46,500. While this is slightly better than the previous deal because you started lower, you should not have split the difference. Being $6K apart, you should actually move up by the $2K they dropped. Now, you are at the low end of your range, $44K. Notice now that if the dealer splits the difference, the deal is at $46K, which you may or may not take. If they initiate the split, the best response is to copy them and split the difference, which would be $45K. Now, the dealer has given up $3K, and you only gave up $1K of the value range.

Great hagglers plan these possibilities out prior to a negotiation. They think through the conversation, wondering, "*If we say this, they might say this or that.*" They have a plan for a response that favors a lower or higher number. Great hagglers aren't afraid of math. They use it to their advantage. Remember and beware, if you are the first to split the difference, you have opened the door to the tactic.

When haggling, you are working on outcome tension. But don't forget the relationship, process, timing, team, and agent tensions. Just because you are haggling doesn't mean you turn the rest of your skills off. If you get stuck at a bid, e.g., they are at $48K and you are at $44K, you can mention that this will be your dealership from now on and that your spouse will need a car soon. You can invoke process or timing and make it clear that you won't buy today unless you can get your price. You can have someone with you (the dealer has a team, after all) or say you need someone else's permission. While you are doing positional math, you can try to insert what *GTY* calls objective criteria. You can show that the average sale of a car of that type is $45,000, for example. The main challenge of using objective criteria commonly occurs during the process of negotiation. The main impediment is that no one rolls over when you introduce objective criteria. After you tell the dealer's salesperson that the Kelly Blue Book on the car is X, they will introduce all the reasons why you can't rely on KBB or argue about the condition of the car or other features. You will find yourself arguing with the seller about the objective criteria. It isn't that you shouldn't introduce this information; you just need to be prepared to argue about the objective criteria. They will have their own book or competitor to KBB to share with you.

Much of negotiation involves positional bargaining. You need to think through and be prepared for mathematical analysis so that when you engage, you have already calculated the likely back and forth. As you negotiate or witness negotiations, you should try to guess the sequence of bids and asks. This takes lots of practice, but you don't have to wait for your own deal. Help others with theirs. It isn't enough to just do factual research on objective criteria, such as average sales prices or authoritative sources. You need to plan for and be prepared for the likely sequences of haggling.

CHAPTER 19

Using the Seven Tensions to Uncover Backstories and Escape Rabbit Holes

SOME OF THE most powerful elements of negotiation are unseen. How often have you negotiated with a party and told your team the other side was irrational or even "crazy"? When you find yourself in this position, it is likely that there is something hidden from you that you don't know or understand. If you knew this thing or understood this element, you may find that your counterparty may actually be very rational.

Therefore, uncovering backstories needs to be a key part of your process planning. There is generally so much going on that is not immediately apparent in a negotiation. Sometimes, information is held back intentionally, and some information is left out because it is seen as irrelevant.

What are Backstories?

Suppose you want to buy a piece of undeveloped land, and you are negotiating with a broker. You know the asking price and that it is owned by a trust. You are aware of the potential development you can build on the land and that the price is negotiable. What you don't know but could probably learn through some due diligence is who the beneficiaries of the trust are. Who really owns the real estate? You don't know the relationship tension. Is it a real estate developer who changed their mind about developing the property? Is it three heirs of a recently deceased billionaire? These questions lead to very different outcome possibilities and negotiation approaches.

The Tool of Provocation to Uncover Backstories

So, how can you uncover the backstory? One option is to simply ask and listen. Ask the broker about the beneficiaries of the trust. If the broker won't tell you, then you may design a negotiating process that will tell you more about the buyer. Maybe you submit a low-ball offer and see the broker's reaction. If asking does not prove to be informative, the seven tensions can help you uncover these hidden stories or elements. Recently, I bought a home. I had heard that the woman who lived in it had died, and her husband had died many years earlier. But I knew nothing else. However, I wanted to know the full backstory, so I became an investigator. I learned that the deceased were extremely wealthy (more billionaires than millionaires). I learned they had two children, and they were living elsewhere and were not involved in the house or transaction. The backstory that developed was that the kids didn't care about the house. It was in disrepair. I knew I could get the house very reasonably because anyone who would care was no longer alive. The kids, I assumed, based on their reported behavior, were very wealthy in their own rights now, and this house was negligible in value compared to their lives. I ended up buying the furniture for a low price as well as getting a good deal on the multi-million-dollar home. That backstory, that "What is really going on?" was extremely important to my negotiation, and it is critical to yours.

I used several tensions to gain this knowledge. First, I developed a really good relationship with the seller's agent. Then, I asked if anyone from the family would be involved. This questioning established who was "in the room," which is an important aspect of process tension. I tested the timing tension by offering the full asking price and a seven-day cash close. They turned down my seven-day close and said thirty was fine. I wondered why, but when I arrived, I found out that it was still full of furniture, which they had to deal with before they could close a deal. So, I immediately made an offer for the furniture to facilitate my own deal. Pushing on the tensions is a highly effective way to discover the backstory.

In another instance, my partner and I needed more real estate space for the aerospace and defense staffing company we owned, which was growing rapidly. Our lease had been signed in the late 1990s, and real estate costs had really dropped. We had two years left on the long-term lease, but we could do what was called a "blend and extend." In a blend and extend, we could renew our lease at a lower rate and then extend the term so the average price was substantially lower than our existing rate. While we were negotiating with our existing landlord, a broker told us a new opportunity had surfaced rather suddenly due to a bankruptcy—that was the first backstory. We quickly went to look at it. We could get this space cheap. It had been vacated rapidly, as there was still coffee in the pots. All the furniture was still there. It was thirty thousand square feet of completely furnished space. I asked the broker about the furniture and the cubicles. He said he didn't know the situation, but they might be available. He told us the first bankruptcy hearing was going to be on Monday, and we agreed to attend, thinking timing tension was on our side.

Come Monday, the broker and I phoned into the hearing. He explained we were interested in the space, and the judge, with the consent of the bankruptcy trustee, granted it to us at a very low lease rate. The gavel dropped on the lease.

I then said, "What about the furniture?"

Nobody from the bankruptcy trustee's office had been to the space, so everyone said, "What furniture?"

I explained that there were cubicles, desks, and related accessories. The judge asked the parties, and they said they would have to look at it.

I said, "No problem. For us to take the lease, we need the furniture removed immediately."

It got quiet. I assumed they were talking. They said, "What will you pay for the furniture?"

Now, I knew they hadn't seen it. The area was outfitted with Herman Miller cubicles that were worth at least one hundred thousand dollars.

I said, "We will pay ten dollars, or we need it removed immediately."

It got quiet again.

The judge asked, "Do you need all of the furniture or just some of it?"

I replied, "We will buy all of it for ten dollars or none of it."

It got quiet again, and then, after some murmuring with the bankruptcy trustee, the judge came back and said, "Okay."

Once I knew they had been too lazy to go see the furniture, I rightly assumed they were too lazy to deal with it. Backstories are critical. Your process planning must include the search for backstories and use the tensions to uncover them.

The Rabbit Hole

From Alice's Adventures in Wonderland, Chapter 6

"Would you tell me, please, which way I ought to go from here?"
"That depends a good deal on where you want to get to,"
said the Cat.
"I don't much care where—," said Alice.
"Then it doesn't matter which way to go," said the Cat.
"—so long as I get somewhere," Alice added as an explanation.

"Oh, you're sure to do that," said the Cat,
"if you only walk long enough."

Every negotiator has caught themselves feeling unhappy with where they ended up in the negotiation. It is like waking up from a bad dream and saying, "Where am I?" or "What am I doing?"

Sometimes, our processes derail. If you have ever seen a video of a train derailment, it happens more slowly than you may realize. Similarly, sometimes, you wake up one moment in the heat of a negotiation and realize it is not going according to plan. Your train has come off the rails.

This is one of the most serious problems with the "let's make a deal" culture. The desire to reach an agreement is so strong that you make a series of concessions in the name of progress, and then you wake up and realize you have fallen down a rabbit hole similar to Alice's. Have you ever been in a negotiation where you were making progress, getting through deal points, and the progress was making you happy? Moreover, your counterparty seemed happy, so all was well. Then, suddenly, you began to get this bad feeling. Some people feel it in their heads, some in their shoulders, and some in their gut. But no matter where you get the feeling, it is for the same reason: you feel regretful. You begin to have deal hesitation and think you have taken a wrong turn. You have agreed to all the points, but now, you have process tension. The process has led you down a rabbit hole, and you want out or, at least, to change your location. What do you do now?

As a board member and officer of the HOA of a luxury high-rise, I fell into a rabbit hole once. When you serve on an HOA of a high-rise, you occasionally face tension from the city and its developers when they build on adjacent properties, which affects the residents' views. When these buildings are in the Central Business District (CBD), there are often very few restrictions on development, but the developers and the city generally want to be good neighbors.

In my building's case, the developer wanted to have a good relationship with the residents of the luxury high-rise. Another officer of the HOA and I undertook a negotiation known as a "good neighbor agreement" with the developer and its representatives. While we got some initial concessions on some minor issues, when we got further into the issues, we hit a stone wall. For example, they acknowledged that we would likely experience some dust, debris, and related construction nuisance issues. They agreed to clean our building's exterior and to pay for our balcony cleanings during the construction. They agreed that we could have a point of contact to quickly escalate complaints. However, heavy-duty issues, like increasing the setback from the street and thereby putting further distance between our buildings, were a no-go. Other issues of importance were also off limits to us, like how traffic would flow during working hours. As the process continued, we agreed to some things because we felt we had no choice. Several tensions descended on us at once. We felt like the outcome was going against us, the process was favoring them, the timing was too quick, and we were powerless. All these tensions began to settle in on my team and me. We looked at each other and began to regret our position. We had been pulled down the proverbial rabbit hole.

When you find yourself down the rabbit hole, it can be a tricky situation. You have agreed to things that you regret. You may fear that if you re-engage on items you already agreed to, your negotiating integrity (aka trust) will evaporate or at least be at risk. Why should they trust you in further negotiations? You have three potential strategies in this situation.

First, you can halt the negotiation and be transparent with your counterparty before retracing your steps. You can explain where you want to begin again. Second, you can exercise outcome tension by deciding to walk away because the deal you are trending toward does not exceed your BATNA.

Then, there is a third option, one they don't teach you in cooperative bargaining training. You can discombobulate your counterparty, which is both a process and a power move. What does discombobulation look like in a negotiation, and why does it work?

In Graduate Business School, I read a great article about changing human behavior in organizations. To understand human behavioral changes, researchers focused on one of the most striking processes that causes behavioral changes in humans. They studied boot camp. The basic question was, "How do we take a sweet eighteen-year-old kid who has been taught throughout their entire childhood not to harm anyone and then teach them to kill on command?" The article identified a three-step process: discombobulation, training, and reinforcement. The discombobulation phase will be recognizable by anyone who has seen any movie or show about boot camp or been through it. In the 1982 film *An Officer and A Gentleman*, for example, the discombobulation began as soon as they arrived. Louis Gossett Jr., the drill sergeant, denigrates each and every one of the new recruits. He calls them "slimy worms." He insults where they are from. He challenges their masculinity. He insults the "college pukes." Next, their heads are shaven. Then, they are woken up early to march, run, and train. This discombobulation puts them in "change mode." Next, they start the training phase and learn various soldier tasks. They are taught to march, shoot, and take apart and put together various weapons. Finally, in phase three, those lessons are reinforced with both rewards and punishments. You do well, and you get to leave. You do poorly, and you get kitchen or latrine duty. Discombobulation, training, and reinforcement make the training stick. You can use these same techniques to turn a negotiation around that has drifted in the wrong direction. I have been on both sides of this technique, and you probably have, too.

How to Know You Have Fallen into a Rabbit Hole

Always stay in touch with your gut feelings as you negotiate. Of all the tensions, I think outcome tension is the easiest to feel, followed by relationship tension. The sinking feeling that you are not going to get that job, that car, or that Snickers bar that you wanted is a good indication that you have fallen down the rabbit hole. A second indication is a disturbance in the relationship. As you feel what you wanted slipping away (outcome tension), you begin to feel worse about the counterparty (relationship tension). Regret is the thought, but tension is the feeling inside. It is often said that a good agreement is one where nobody is happy. What a stupid quote. That comes from the same school of thought that says all deals should be win-win.

Methods to Find Your Way Out

So, here we were, a fellow board member and I, trying to negotiate a "good neighbor agreement." After negotiating for a while and feeling like they didn't care about us as neighbors, we thought, *Now what?* As I said earlier, you only have three options. Retracing our steps with them didn't seem like a good move because they would simply be happy with how things had gone, and retracing would further cement their position. They didn't need our approval for anything from a legal perspective, so walking away would mean we would get nothing. I pondered how to pass our tension to them. I wanted them to feel like we felt.

So, I invited them to a party at my condo, which was going to be directly affected by their work. I made sure my wife and team member from the board would be there. I said, "Hey, let's get a start on the new neighborhood with some drinks and sushi at my condo." Wanting to show they could be good neighbors, they all agreed to attend. I served some terrific wine and appetizers. Their lot was perfectly visible, and their building could easily be imagined. As much as I wanted to chat with them about matters, they were all glued to the window, imagining the building and its impact on our residents. They could look down at the street and imagine the traffic. They could imagine the dust, noise, and light from the construction. Man, were they discombobulated. They stared and stared. They literally couldn't help but see the world through our eyes. They became tense. They began to have ideas as a result of the tension. By the next meeting, they had a whole new wave of ideas to mitigate the construction's impact and work with us to be good neighbors.

The moral of the story is obvious. As soon as they came into our home, they felt our tension. One of the most powerful feelings we have is of "home." Imagine how discombobulating it was for them to see their work from our home. When you have trouble getting someone to share your tension, find a home to bring them to. Never underestimate the power of the physical. In your arsenal of tools to deal with process tension, never forget the impact of the location. Field trips can be very powerful.

I recall another time when a resident complained of vibrations in their unit. Vibrations are common in large buildings, and condo documents always have a disclaimer regarding the reality of high-rise residential life. We had measurements that indicated that the tremors were within the zone of acceptable vibrations. I thought I understood the cause of the vibrations and some things we could do to mitigate them further, but one day, the engineer who served on our board called me and said, "Let's go on a field trip." We met in the parking garage at a joint that was at issue. He showed me there was a space, and one slab was higher than the other. The slab was flexible, and so there was a combination of factors at work. The transfer of weight from one flexible slab to the other caused some vibration. The difference in height was another factor, and the connection of the flexible garage to the static building led to the vibration. The field trip opened my eyes. Although the situation was within legally acceptable tolerances, there were things we could do to improve the issue, primarily by slowing the cars with speed bumps and speed limits. Seeing it in person and understanding it changed my attitude from "it is legally fine" to "let's improve the situation."

You can use the seven tensions to help you with advanced challenges, such as uncovering backstories and escaping from rabbit holes. You might even find yourself on the other side of these seven tension techniques. Have you ever been in a negotiation where the other side seemed to "blow up" out of nowhere? Maybe they dramatically stomped out of a negotiation, and you and your team were left trying to figure out what happened. This was someone discombobulating you with power and process tension. Be mindful of these techniques so you can recognize them and use them to your advantage.

CHAPTER 20

Conclusion: Negotiating with Strength and Without Regret

LIKE MOST DICHOTOMIES, THE line drawn between positional and collaborative negotiation is improper and, at a minimum, overstated. The principles of *Getting to Yes* are helpful process/outcome points but miss much of the matter of negotiating. Negotiation is a human social process that arises from conflict. As such, to understand, undertake, analyze, and teach negotiation, we need to assess the impact of that conflict and the tensions that it brings. Being in touch with and training those tensions leads to successful negotiation by allowing a participant to "flip the script" and force the other party to make the tough decisions.

We have been taught to suppress tension so we don't "lose our temper" or explode due to the distress of tension. But tension is natural, and we need to be in touch with it, not avoid it, to engage civilly with each other in our negotiations.

Based on my study, teaching, and experience, I have posited seven tensions associated with negotiating: relationship, outcome, process, timing, power, team, and agent. If we place an item of value in front of two people, the simplest form of a negotiation problem, these tensions appear. Who is across from me, and what is my relationship with them? What is my desired outcome? What process will I/we use to come to a resolution to the conflict? How is time a factor? Does one of us have leverage over the other? Do I have a team or other constituents? Do they? Is this something I will handle myself, or should I have an agent handle this for me? What if I am the agent?

In the appendices, I have provided some guidance to assist you in preparing for a negotiation, checking on these tensions mid-stream, and evaluating your negotiation. You can improve your negotiating skills tremendously by religiously preparing for the seven tensions, evaluating those tensions, and reflecting on them after each and every negotiation.

What if the world we are in is the result of denying our tensions? What if our conflicts innately lead to tension, and we are not trained to manage and cope with it? What if we changed that? That is my goal and the goal of this book.

Understanding the tensions that flow from conflict, a mastery of them, and the growth that would come from further study could change the world. We need to understand people and their role in the problem. We need to get better at designing resolution processes. We need a better understanding of the role of timing. We need to better understand what outcomes are possible and what can be expected. We need to understand power, its sources, and how to confront it. We need agents. We need to be better agents and learn to collaborate with our teams and cultures. We can change the world by mastering the seven tensions.

APPENDIX A

The Seven Tensions of Negotiation Preparation Template

Relationship Tension

- Who is/are my counterparty/ies?
- Do I know them? If not, how can I get to know them? Do I know anyone who does know them?
- Do we have an existing relationship? Do we have any duties to each other?
- Is this a single transaction relationship, or will there be an ongoing relationship? If it will be ongoing, what type of relationship will it be? What do I want them to think of me/us? Will they be inferior or superior to me in an organization? Will they be my peers?
- Can they affect my reputation? Can I affect theirs?

Outcome Tension

- What do I think I want?
- Why do I think I want that? What is underneath my desire for it?
- How could I get that? How many ways can I think of to get it?
- If I want more than one thing, can I prioritize or rank them?
- What is the best outcome for me/us?
- What is the worst outcome for me/us?
- Do I see any obvious tradeable items?
- What if there is no deal or settlement?
- What do I think they want?
- Why do I think they want that?
- What is their underlying motivation?
- How can they get what they want?
- At what points do our wants conflict?
- Do we have any common goals?
- How would I/we define success?

Leverage Tension

- What power or control do they have over anything I/we want?
- Do they control any of the inputs to what I/we want?
- Regarding any outcome conflicts, who has greater power, me/we or them?
- Can they hurt me/we, our outcome desires, or my/our reputation?
- Can I hurt them, their outcome desires, or their reputation?

Timing Tension

- Does it matter when this deal happens or when the matter gets resolved?
- Who does timing favor?
- Does who timing favors change over time?
- What does the timing curve look like?
- Can I change who timing favors by waiting or hurrying?

Process Tension

- Will we have a meeting, a phone call, and/or an email?
- Where will we meet if we meet? Should we meet on our home court, theirs, or neutral ground?
- Who will I/we include?
- How long will we meet?
- Will we meet more than once?
- Should we break the issues down so we handle some at one meeting and some at another?
- Should we handle the hard ones first or the soft ones?
- Who should make the first offer?
- If I get an offer, should I counter or wait?
- Should we have a discussion about the process before we meet?
- What is our impasse strategy?
- Do we need to involve a third party? A mediator? A facilitator?

Team Tension

- Who is on my team? Who do I need to include?
- Who or what is my broader community?
- Who should I include in what?
- Who do I need to keep updated? How will I do that?
- What authority do I have?
- What authority am I willing to delegate? To whom?

Agent Tension

- Do I need an agent? A lawyer? A broker?
- Do I need a subject matter expert? An accountant or other professional?
- If I am an agent, what authority do I have as an agent?
- What authority do I need to reach a deal or resolve a dispute?
- Does my agent have any potential conflicts of interest, even "light" conflicts of interest?
- How often do I want my agent to consult with me?
- How will I monitor the success of my agent?
- Under what conditions would I replace my agent?
- If I am an agent, how will I explain success or failure to my client/principal?

APPENDIX B

The Seven Tensions of Negotiation
Mid-Negotiation Gut Checks

Relationship Tension

- Have I discovered any new counterparties? Are some more important than others? Have I refined who the decision maker is?

- How is the relationship developing? Am I getting to know them? Have I continued to scan my network for connections? Any feedback from them? Were my connections accurate in their assessment?

- In the case of an existing relationship, have I improved it, damaged it, or not changed it? What, if anything new, have I learned about them? If we have any duties to each other, are they being honored?

- If this is a single-transaction relationship, have I learned anything that would make me want to seek a further relationship? If there will be any ongoing relationship, what do I think they think of me? What do I think of them? Is there alignment in our perceptions of each other?

- Have I engaged with them socially? How was that? Did I learn anything "outside the conference room?"
- Can I find out what they are saying about me to others? What am I saying to others about them? How are we advancing or damaging each other's reputation?

Outcome Tension

- Have I clarified what I want by asking myself why I want it and how I am going to get it?
- Has what I want changed from when we began negotiations?
- Have I prioritized and/or ranked what I want?
- What percentage of my best outcome for me/us have I achieved or expect to achieve?
- Have new downsides surfaced? Is there a worse outcome for me/us that I hadn't identified initially?
- Have I identified, clarified, or initiated a trade of any tradeable items?
- Have I clearly confirmed my alternatives if there is no deal? Have I secured options or other rights so I know I have alternatives?
- Has what they wanted changed in any respect?
- Have I asked why they think they want what they want?
- Have I discovered and/or clarified their underlying motivation?
- Have they confirmed the "how" of getting what they want?

- What are the conflict points I/we have identified? Have we designed a process for addressing them?
- Have we identified any common goals? Are their priorities on conflict points and common points different than mine?
- Are we more on a success or failure trajectory?

Leverage Tension

- Have they threatened me/us on any point?
- Have they clarified the power or control they have over anything I/we want?
- Have they clarified the power or control they have over any of the inputs to what I/we want?
- Have we threatened them in any respect?
- Regarding any conflicts, what have I/we learned about who has greater power, me/we or them?
- Have I better identified how they can hurt me/we, our outcome desires, or my/our reputation?
- Have I better identified how I can hurt them, their outcome desires, or their reputation?

Timing Tension

- Am I feeling any time pressure as to when this deal happens or the matter gets resolved?
- Do I sense they are feeling any time pressure as to when this deal happens or the matter gets resolved?
- Has who timing favors changed over time?
- What does the future timing curve look like?

- Based on the timing factors, should I accelerate or decelerate? Should I lead or drag?

Process Tension

- How many engagements have we had? How would I rate them? Do we tend to do better in physical meetings, Zoom, or phone calls?
- How many more engagements do we need? What have I learned from our engagements?
- Where have we been meeting if we have met? Has the place mattered in the meeting?
- Who have I/we included? Is there any desire to change the team or who is in the room? How would I rate the performance of the team and its individuals? How would I rate my performance so far?
- Who have they included? Is there anyone I want on or off of their team or out of the room?
- How long are the meetings lasting? Are they productive?
- Are some issues lagging? Should we handle them at a special meeting?
- Have we been leaning toward resolving the hard or the soft issues?
- Where are we in the offer/counteroffer exchanges? Have we developed a natural rhythm?
- Do we need another meeting about the process to design the endgame?
- Have we developed any impasses? What is the plan for any deadlocks?

- Do we need to involve a third party? A mediator? A facilitator?
- Am I building in subsequent dispute resolution mechanisms?

Team Tension

- Am I happy with how the team is working together? Is the team happy with the leadership? Are there tensions between team members? Have coalitions formed?
- Do I perceive issues with their team, its leadership, or internal tensions?
- What is the perception or feedback from my broader community?
- Is anyone feeling underappreciated? Is anyone dominating?
- Am I updating who I need? How often am I doing that?
- Am I exceeding my authority? Do I need more authority?
- What authority am I delegating? To whom? How are they doing?

Agent Tension

- Did I hire an agent? A lawyer? A broker? How is that working?
- Did I hire a subject matter expert? An accountant or other professional? How is that working?
- If I am an agent, how am I doing?
- Do I need more authority to reach a deal or resolve a dispute?

- Does my agent have any potential conflicts of interest, even "light" conflicts of interest?
- How often does my agent consult with me?
- Is my agent succeeding?
- Under what conditions would I replace my agent?
- If I am an agent, how will I explain success or failure to my client/principal?

APPENDIX C

The Seven Tensions of Negotiation
Post-Negotiation Reflection
and Corrective Actions

Relationship Tension

- How would I rate how I handled my counterparty/ies? How would I rate how they handled me/us?
- If I knew them, what did I learn about them that I didn't know before? How would I handle them differently next time based on what I learned? Would I want to deal with them again? Would they want to deal with me/us again?
- What is one thing I got wrong about them? What did they get wrong about me? Can or should we do a debrief informally or formally?
- How accurate were my network sources with respect to someone I didn't know? Any need to reach out and share divergences with what I/we were told?

- How did our existing relationship change if we had one? If there were any duties owed to each other, were they honored? How well?
- If this was a single-transaction relationship, what did I learn about this type of engagement that will help me with similar styles or cultures? In an ongoing relationship, how is the relationship now? Is it better, worse, the same, or different in any other way? What do I think they think of me/us now?
- Will it be hard to work together, whether they are to be inferior or superior to me in an organization or my peer? Is there anything I need to do to repair the relationship? Should we have a celebration dinner, drinks, or ceremony?
- How will the outcome and process affect my reputation? Theirs?

Outcome Tension

- What was the result? Did I resolve the underlying desire and motivation with the result? Is anything still open?
- After some time, do I/we want to revisit anything?
- Do I/we foresee any problems with the execution of the provisions? Are my dispute resolution routes clear and solid?
- If I/we wanted more than one thing, did we get results that aligned with our priorities?
- How close did we come to the best outcome for me/us?
- How close did we come to the worst outcome for me/us?
- Did we make any good trades? Any regrets about those?

- If there was no deal or settlement, can I clearly articulate the reason to my team, community, or client?
- Did they get what they wanted?
- Did I/we fully learn their underlying motivation?
- At points of conflict, did we resolve them? How? Any lessons for the future?
- Were our common goals achieved in a mutually beneficial way?
- Were we successful based on how we defined success?

Leverage Tension

- How did power or control affect the outcome?
- Did they control any of the inputs we needed?
- Who did a better job wielding or leveraging the power they had, me/we or them?
- Did they damage our outcome desires or my/our reputation?
- Did I damage their outcome desires or their reputation?

Timing Tension

- Did timing matter for when this deal happened or when the matter got resolved?
- Who did timing favor?
- Did who timing favored change over time?
- How would I draft the power/timing curve now that it is over?
- How well did we use waiting and/or hurrying?
- What did I learn about timing and its use in negotiations?
- What will I do differently next time?

Process Tension

- What modes of communication did we use? Do I have any regrets about the modes of communication I used? Did I learn any lessons for next time?
- Where did we meet if we met? Did we meet on our home court, theirs, or neutral ground? Any regrets about the meetings? Did I learn any lessons?
- Who did we include? Did we have the right players?
- How long did we meet? Was the allocated time enough? Were there any rushed decisions?
- Did we meet more than once? How was the number of meetings? Did I learn any lessons?
- Did we segment the issues? How did that work? Did we have focus meetings or focus groups working on the issues?
- Did we handle the hard issues first or the soft ones? What did I learn from that? Do we need to emphasize dealing with the big issues up front? Or were we comfortable easing into the hard issues after some soft issues?
- Who made the first offer? Why? How did the other party react?
- Did we or did they counter or wait?
- Did we have a meeting about the process before we met? Did we follow any agreed-upon plan for the process?
- When we reached impasses, how did our impasse strategy work?
- Did we involve a third party? A mediator? A facilitator? Were they effective?

Team Tension

- Who was on my team? Any regrets or lessons learned about the team makeup? Did we get feedback from our broader community? Did they? Did we get community pressure? Did we give any community pressure?
- Did we assign duties thoughtfully? Any regrets about who we included in what?
- Did I update my constituents properly? How did I do that? Any lessons learned?
- What authority did I have? Did I have enough? Did I use all I had?
- Did I delegate? To whom? Did I give my team the power it needed?

Agency Tension

- Did I retain an agent? A lawyer? A broker?
- Did I retain a subject matter expert? An accountant or other professional?
- If I was an agent, what authority did I have as an agent? Did I use all of it? Did I need more?
- What authority did I need to reach a deal or resolve a dispute? Did I have it?
- Did my agent have any potential conflicts of interest, even "light" conflicts of interest? Did they surface?
- Did my agent consult with me? Often enough? Too much?
- How would I rate the success of my agent?
- Did I replace my agent? Should I have replaced my agent?
- How will I explain success or failure to my client/principal?

APPENDIX D

Suggested Topics and Questions for Common Links Regarding My Counterparty (MC)

THESE QUESTIONS ARE just to get you started if you need some ideas when interviewing people within your network about your counterparty. The specific context of your negotiation may cause you to have additional questions. The important thing is that you don't just "wing" the conversation but approach it in a structured fashion. You will also want to pay attention to the answers so you make solid follow-up questions. I recommend updating your template with questions and follow-up questions that might be helpful in the future.

- How do you know MC? How did you meet? Do you know them personally or professionally?
- If personally, what are their hobbies or sports of interest?
- Are they introverted or extroverted?

- If professionally, have you ever been in a meeting with them? Do they tend to lead?
- Are they a better talker or listener or balanced?
- How would you describe MC's negotiating style? Aggressive, passive, or in the middle?
- Are they open-minded, opinionated, or balanced?
- Are they more planning-oriented or spontaneous?
- Are they more factual and scientific or intuitive and instinctive?
- If they are an intermediary, what types of clients do they usually represent?
- Do you know anyone else that I could speak with about them?

APPENDIX E

The Seven Tensions Agent Alignment Template

I. Relationship Tension: What is our relationship going to be? Are we going to be friends? Will there be a social aspect? What do I want the relationship to be? Formal? Informal?

II. Outcome Tension: What is the objective of the representation? What do I want the agent to get for me?

III. Process Tension: What steps will the agent take on my behalf? What are the ground rules for the engagement? What will the agent do, and what will I do? What are the mileposts we can agree on in advance?

IV. Power Tension: What are our levers? What is our strength? What is our weakness? How will we play those?

V. Timing Tension: When do I want this done? What is the timing of the various mileposts?

VI. Team Tension: Who else on my side does the agent need to keep involved or seek affirmation from in my absence?

VII. Agent Tension: What is the scope of the representation? How will I judge the success of the agent?

BIBLIOGRAPHY

1. Ambady, N., and R. Rosenthal. "Judging Social Behavior Using 'Thin Slices.' " CHANCE, 1997, 10(4), 12–51. https://doi-org.libproxy .wustl.edu/10.1080/09332480.1997.10542056.

2. Bahney, Anna. "After a $1.8 billion verdict, the clock is ticking on the 6% real estate commission." CNN, 5 Nov. 2023.

3. "Condominium Act." *Condominium Act - Uniform Law Commission*, www.uniformlaws.org/committees/community-home?Community Key=3304f481-3a47-4f52-9b05-73db978e33bc. Accessed 10 Sept. 2024.

4. "Deaths in Wars and Conflicts in the 20th Century." *Center for International and Security Studies at Maryland*, University of Maryland School of Public Policy, cissm.umd.edu/research-impact/publications /deaths-wars-and-conflicts-20th-century. Accessed 5 Jan. 2024.

5. DeVito, Alessandra. "Why We're Drawn to People Who Are Similar to Us." *PSYCH 424 Blog*, sites.psu.edu/aspsy/2024/04/05/why-were -drawn-to-people-who-are-similar-to-us/#:~:text=One%20of%20 the%20thing%20behind,reinforces%20our%20sense%20of%20 identity.

6. Fisher, Roger, and William Ury. *Getting to Yes*. Boston, Houghton Mifflin, 1981.

7. Hilty, John A, and Peter J. Carnevale. "Black-Hat/White-Hat Strategy in Bilateral Negotiation." Organizational Behavior and Human Decision Processes, Vol 55, Issue 3, August 1993 pp 444-469.

8. Kulshreshtha, Ambar, et al. "Association of Perceived Stress with Cognition among Older US Adults." *JAMA Network Open*, JAMA Network, 7 Mar. 2023, jamanetwork.com/journals/jamanetworkopen/fullarticle/2802090.

9. "Legal Services: Litigation Spending in the U.S. 2015-2021." *Statista*, Statista Research Department, 6 July 2022, www.statista.com/statistics/941275/litigation-spending-united-states/.

10. Mezrich, Ben. "Breaking Twitter: Elon Musk and the Most Controversial Corporate Takeover in History." Grand Central Publishing, 7 Nov. 2023.

11. Morris, Chris. "Business Travel, Just like Almost Everything from Pre-Covid Life, Is Going Back to Normal." *Fortune*, Fortune, 15 Aug. 2023, fortune.com/2023/08/15/business-travel-spending-2023-post pandemic-covid-returning-to-normal/.

12. Murphy, Nora A, and Judith A. Hall. "Capturing Behavior in Small Doses: A Review of Comparative Research in Evaluating Thin Slices for Behavioral Measurement." Frontiers in Psychology, April 29, 2021, www.ncbi.nlm.nih.gov/pmc/articles/PMC8116694/.

13. PON Staff. "3 Types of Power in Negotiation." *Daily Blog*, Program on Negotiation Harvard Law School, 13 Aug. 2024, https://www.pon.har vard.edu/daily/negotiation-skills-daily/types-of-power-in-negotia tion/.

14. PON Staff. "Negotiations and Logrolling: Discover Opportunities to Generate Mutual Gains." *PON*, 6 May 2024, www.pon.harvard .edu/daily/mediation/mediation-breaking-a-partial-impasse-in-nego tiations/#:~:text=In%20negotiation%2C%20logrolling%20is%20 the,for%20a%20treasured%20dining%20table.

15. Shonk, Katie. "Conflict-Solving Strategies: The Value of Taking a Break." *PON*, 12 Apr. 2019, www.pon.harvard.edu/daily/conflict-resolution /conflict-solving-strategies-the-value-of-taking-a-break/.

16. Spacey, John. "4 Types of Negotiating Power." Simplicable, 15 Aug. 2017, https://simplicable.com/new/negotiating-power.

17. "Timeline of billionaire Elon Musk's bid to control Twitter." The Associated Press, 28 Oct. 2022, apnews.com/article/twitter -elon-musk-timeline-c6b09620ee0905e59df9325ed042a609.

18. Tversky, Amos, and Daniel Kahneman. *Judgment under Uncertainty: Heuristics and Biases*, American Association for the Advancement of Science, 27 Sept. 1974, www2.psych.ubc.ca/~schaller/Psyc590 Readings/TverskyKahneman1974.pdf.

ABOUT THE AUTHOR

 Steven "Cash" Nickerson is Chairman & CEO of Nickerson Stoneleigh, Inc., a private investment firm he founded with its headquarters in Dallas, Texas. He is also President of Cash Nickerson, P.C., a law and negotiation consulting firm. He was Chairman of North America of AKKA Technologies, SE, based in Brussels, Belgium, prior to its sale to Adecco SA, based in Zurich, Switzerland. Cash was President, CFO, General Counsel, and the second largest shareholder of PDS Tech, Inc. prior to its sale to AKKA Technologies, SE. Other previous roles include corporate attorney and marketing executive for Union Pacific Railroad, associate and then a partner at Am Law 200 law firm Jenner & Block, and Chairman and

CEO of a tech company. Mr. Nickerson, author of seven books, is an avid writer and speaker on negotiation, the workplace, jobs, and the economy. Mr. Nickerson is the founder and president of the David H. Nickerson Foundation, which supports prostate cancer research.

In addition to his leadership on the Board of Trustees, Mr. Nickerson serves on the Advisory Board of the School of Law and is a member of the International Council at the Whitney R. Harris World Law Institute. He is chair of both the Dallas-Fort Worth and Austin-San Antonio Regional Cabinets and chaired the North and Central Texas Regional Campaign for Leading Together: The Campaign for Washington University. Mr. Nickerson is a recipient of the Dallas-Fort Worth Regional Award (2009), the Global Philanthropy Award for the Harris Institute Crimes Against Humanity Initiative (2010), the School of Law Distinguished Alumni Award (2013), and the Founders Day Distinguished Alumni Award (2014). Mr. Nickerson earned his BA from Carleton College and his MBA and JD from Washington University in St. Louis, where he was an editor of the law review. He is currently a JSD candidate and an adjunct faculty member at WashULaw, teaching Business Lawyering and Negotiation.